CONCILIUM

THEOLOGY IN THE AGE OF RENEWAL

CONCILIUM

CONCILIUM/VOL. 41

DOGMA

THE PROBLEM OF ESCHATOLOGY

edited by EDWARD SCHILLEBEECKX, O.P.
BONIFACE WILLEMS, O.P.

VOLUME 41

CONCILIUM
theology in the age of renewal

PAULIST PRESS
NEW YORK, N.Y. / GLEN ROCK, N.J.

236
P962s

PAULIST PRESS
EXECUTIVE OFFICES: 304 W. 58th Street, New York, N.Y. and 21 Harris-
    town Road, Glen Rock, N.J.
Publisher: John A. Carr, C.S.P.

EDITORIAL OFFICES: 304 W. 58th Street, New York, N.Y.
Executive Editor: Kevin A. Lynch, C.S.P.
Managing Editor: Urban P. Intondi

Printed and bound in the United States of America by
Wickersham Printing Co., Lancaster, Pa.

201684

CONTENTS

PART II

BIBLIOGRAPHICAL SURVEY

PART III

DOCUMENTATION CONCILIUM
Office of the Executive Secretary
Nijmegen, Netherlands

PREFACE

Edward Schillebeeckx, O.P./*Nijmegen, Netherlands*
Boniface Willems, O.P./*Nijmegen, Netherlands*

Many priests today find it difficult to talk about eschatological topics. Yet the official documents of the magisterium, particularly the texts of Vatican Council II, stress the eschatological dimension of our salvation. Why then this gap between the official teaching and ordinary practice? The reason is probably that in their day-to-day preaching priests feel that their task is to keep as close as possible to the way in which the ordinary faithful experience their concrete existence. It would appear rather difficult to speak about eschatological subjects in such a way that the people, living in a de-mythologized society, can fit these subjects into their daily life and experience. It is as if we have lost the terminology, the "categories", which would enable us to speak also about the "supraworldly" dimension of our salvation.

One of the basic questions, therefore, which recurs in several articles of this volume of *Concilium* is whether the eschatological aspect of our salvation—i.e., the aspect which concerns the ultimate future—is purely "beyond this world" or whether it also has significance for this present world. The searching discussions with the Marxists about man's expectations of the future have made our present generation of Christians more sensitive to the reproach that our preaching of the hereafter has caused the faithful to neglect their earthly responsibilities in the sometimes pietistic hope of a happy future which exists somewhere verti-cally above our present condition. This objection, which is con-stantly gaining in force, is an essential aspect of most of the articles in this volume. Some of the authors have even placed it right in the forefront of their discussion.

If formerly, in our reflection on death, the attention went straight to life after death, modern discussions about death begin by analyzing the meaning of death for our present life in its historical situation. The climate of our understanding has clearly undergone a change. Theology, as the preliminary condition of preaching, must therefore not only voice the Church's under-standing to the world but also the world's understanding to the Church. In the changed climate of understanding, theology must examine the faith anew, and so this faith needs constant and new reflection. But this new reflection upon the faith is not only *criti-cally* involved in the new mentality but remains subject to the message of the Gospel as its sovereign norm. It is in this perspec-tive that the contributors to this volume have tried to clarify the way in which modern man can understand some eschatological dogmas as a help toward the intelligible preaching of our escha-tological salvation.

One of the consequences of this pastoral concern is that these articles are more explicitly biblical in treatment than is usually the case in explanations of dogma. The aim is to discover the "original" meaning of the ecclesiastical formulas as they devel-oped in the course of Church history in order to penetrate to the primitive heart of the eschatological message. This process, nec-essary for all contemporary preaching, has been called "de-mythologization", a technical term which seems to upset some people. The reality expressed by this process is necessary for a living Church that cannot rest satisfied with the mechanical repe-tition of the old message but has to present Christ's salvation as something that is permanently actual. The words are new, and up to a certain point this is also true of the reflection, but the reality of this process is already operative in the Bible itself and is there-fore found in every period of the Church's history.

Because eschatology has long remained a kind of underdeveloped region in ecclesiastical thought, our generation particularly needs an intensive, faith-inspired investigation in this field. This investigation and this new reflection must not remain limited to professional theologians. The priests who are in immediate contact with the people must also make their contribution. If they do not, they will find—as a fair number have already discovered—that there is an important part of Christian salvation about which they are basically ignorant.

This volume of *Concilium* seeks to help all those who are directly involved in this preaching. It begins with an explicitly biblical contribution by George which gives a careful study of one facet of the eschatological dogma—namely, God's judgment. But this study of the real meaning of God's judgment shows that preaching this judgment is not merely concerned with the end of time, but that it summons the Christian particularly to faithfulness to God here and now. As has already been said above, it is very important to see the connection between the way in which eschatological thought was formulated in a given age and the social and cultural conditions of that age. In this way one begins to understand the time-conditioned and therefore relative aspects in which the basic meaning was discussed (Müller-Goldkuhle). It then appears, for instance, that there is a definite link between the fading of the eschatological expectation and the institutionalization of the community of believers.

As time proceeds, however, we have to find a new balance between the necessary institutionalization of the Church and the dynamic striving toward the future of the community. A hermeneutical article shows that the community understood history as a history of tradition and so saw historical events as part of a promise concerning the future in such a way that earthly history itself becomes an unveiling of an eschatological expectation for the believer. Therefore we can say nothing about the ultimate things (the *eschata*), such as the resurrection, the judgment, the parousia and eternal life, *except insofar as* these events are already initiated in the course of history as God's activity in and through the covenant (Schillebeeckx). History, however, is ambivalent and has no definite and single interpretation. Is it then merely "a tale told by an idiot", as Macbeth believed? This ambivalence is examined by Castelli Gattinara di Zubiena who, starting from the concept of "sign", sees it as the negation of immediacy. He concludes that history *is* in fact something different from what it appears to be in its immediacy, even though we cannot prove this by rational argument.

From these considerations of a more general nature the contents of this volume pass on to the clarification of some specific aspects of our eschatology: the "separated soul", the resurrection and eternal life. Since we have abandoned the heavily dualistic understanding of man of earlier days, the Christian belief in a hereafter now has to answer questions about whether there is any sense in speaking about a "soul separated from the body". This traditional presupposition will therefore have to be "de-mythologized", but this must be done in such a way that the real meaning of the Church's teaching is fully brought out (González-Ruiz). The dogma of the resurrection, especially, has been treated by Bultmann and his followers in such a way that one begins to wonder whether these interpretations still fully preserve the original biblical meaning of this central point of the Christian kerygma.

In this controversy Schlier has entered the lists on the Catholic side. Paul said that without the resurrection of the Lord Jesus, the Christian faith is vain. In terms of biblical understanding the resurrection is a "dabar" (word)—i.e., a real event which has its place in the language of faith. The event of the resurrection, achieved in Jesus himself, and the growth of belief in the resurrection are not identical, but neither can they be separated as if we could approach the resurrection in terms of historical criticism like any other objective, purely human event. It is only within the faith in the resurrection that the risen Lord can really enter into our earthly history (Grabner-Haider).

Belief in eternal life is therefore a key point in the Christian message. But because this salvation is really incorporated in our history, it must also have a meaning for this earthly history and be of permanent value within the scope of our life on this earth. Only when the earthly significance of the belief in eternal life becomes clear will the proper meaning of eternal life become more intelligible to the modern understanding of the faith (Schoonenberg).

To answer the question whether the eschatological hope of an eternal life is an exclusively Christian interpretation of life, we could only make a choice from the many existing eschatological religions. Although Hinduism has passed through a whole development in its belief about the future, a development that has moved in various directions, its modern phase links its belief in eternal life more and more with the vision of a better future for mankind on this earth (Rayan). The rediscovery of the importance of an eschatological hope for our secular life on this earth has brought Christians and Marxists together to discuss the "absolute future" as a topic acceptable to both sides. A survey of this dialogue is given in this volume by Sauter.

In conclusion, Flanagan presents an outline of the Christian eschatological expectations of the Church in the figure of Mary the mother of Jesus, in whom we find an exemplar of the christological dogma of the *eschaton* as in an "icon": Mary as the image of the future Church.

PART I
ARTICLES

Augustin George, S.M./*Lyon, France*

The Judgment
of God

From the days of the Old Testament to the days of the New Testament, the People of God had their gaze directed toward the future. This is one of the traits that distinguished them from the surrounding nations. While the latter lived in the closed circle of perpetually recurring natural cycles, Israel was ever directed toward the salvation that was to come, and she found a pledge of this coming salvation in God's past interventions, in salvation history.

From age to age her prophets proclaimed this salvation at the imminent end of the present era; that is why their oracles can be called "eschatological". [1] They gave it different names: the Day of Yahweh, the Judgment, the coming of the Messiah, the kingdom of God, the new Jerusalem, the Resurrection. And to describe these events which far surpassed the present state of things, they drew their images from the wondrous deeds of past salvation history, from the mythical cosmology of surrounding nations, and from their experience of an encounter with God.

In attempting to interpret these varied and mysterious depictions, we would do well to pinpoint the source of their images. It would also be wise for us to start out by appreciating the basic

[1] We use the term "eschatological" in the broad sense that most Old Testament theologies give it (i.e., "relating to the end of the present epoch"). Some apply it only to apocalyptic oracles that announce the transformation of the present world into the new cosmos.

aim of each prophet who utilized them. The context in which he
worked and the overall import of his message will thus enable us
to grasp his understanding of the eschatological event—both the
concrete agents of this event and the promises and duties that it
entails.

Since we could not hope to examine all the themes of eschatology within the scope of our present article, we shall here simply examine the meaning which the prophets and Jesus attached
to their predictions of divine judgment.

I

THE OLD TESTAMENT

The "judgment of God" is a theme which appears in all the
prophets in some form or other. One of the classic formulations
of this theme is the "Day of Yahweh". We shall first study the
prophetic statements of this theme, and then we shall examine
the "judgment of God" in the Apocalypse of Daniel, because this
book represents the ultimate statement of Old Testament reflection on this theme.

The Day of Yahweh in the Prophets [2]

The oldest biblical oracle on the Day of Yahweh is that of
Amos (5, 18-20). It dates from the 8th century B.C., when the
northern kingdom was enjoying its last days of prosperity.

The oracle indicates that the people were looking forward to
this day as a time of happiness and prosperity. They undoubtedly
pictured it as being similar to the "day of Madian", when Yahweh gave victory to Gideon (Is. 9, 3), or to the "day when the
Lord delivered up the Amorites to the Israelites" at Gabaon
(Jos. 10, 12-14). This popular expectation, however, represents

[2] On the Day of Yahweh theme, we recommend the articles of A.
Gelin, "Jours de Yahvé et Jour de Yahvé," in *Lumière et Vie* 11 (1953),
pp. 40-52; M. Delcor, "Jour de Yahvé," in *Catholicisme* VI (1965), pp.
1054-58.

a distortion of the real meaning of the covenant. It is a carnal conception in which God's covenant is viewed as an assurance of temporal well-being requiring no deep fidelity on their part.

Amos talks out against this self-centered brand of religion. He proclaims the Day of Yahweh as a day of "darkness", a day of utter catastrophe. The image itself is vague, but the rest of the prophet's message helps us to grasp its import. Throughout his oracles Amos announces the judgment of God against the sinfulness of his people and the surrounding nations (1—2), and he predicts God's imminent chastisement of them. It will involve invasion (3, 11; 6, 14), rout (2, 14-16), destruction (3, 14-15), massacre (5, 16-17; 6, 9-10; 7, 17; 8, 3. 10; 9, 1-4) and exile (4, 2-3; 5, 5. 11. 26-27; 6, 7; 7, 17); only a small "remnant" will be spared (3, 12; 5, 15; 9, 8). Amos obviously envisions an invasion by the armies of Assyria (6, 14; 5, 27), which is already well on its way to becoming lord of the Near East (6, 2). The judgment of God works itself out in history.

Amos is more concerned with spelling out the significance of the day than with describing it in detail. The cause of this catastrophe is to be found in their infidelities to the covenant: the injustice of the great, who live in luxury (3, 10-12. 15; 4, 1-3; 6, 1-11) but oppress the poor (2, 6-7; 4, 1; 5, 7. 10-13; 8, 4-7), and the distorted and superstitious worship that takes place in their sanctuaries (4, 4-5; 5, 5. 21-25).

Challenging their self-centered notion of the covenant, Amos reminds the Israelites of their covenant obligations to God (3, 1-2; 9, 7-8). For him the terrible panorama of imminent catastrophe is essentially a summons to undergo conversion, to do justice to the poor and to offer Yahweh a cult that befits his grandeur (5, 4-6. 14-15. 23-25). His proclamation of the impending day is meant to restore fidelity to the covenant now rather than to describe the future.

We find an analogous meaning in the announcements of the Day of Yahweh by subsequent prophets. Shortly after Amos, in the kingdom of Judah, Isaiah (2, 9-21) stresses the awesome transcendence of Yahweh's appearance, but his other oracles clearly designate Assyria as the rod of God's anger (7, 18. 20; 8, 17; 10, 5).

Isaiah, too, denounces Israel's sinfulness. Like Amos, he speaks out against the luxury of the nobility (2, 7. 12-16; 3, 16-24; 5, 8-14. 22) and the oppression of the poor (1, 17. 23; 3, 1-15; 5, 7-23; 10, 1-2; 29, 21), but he particularly attacks superficial religion (29, 13) and their lack of faith (5, 18-19; 6, 9-10; 7, 13; 19, 9-12; 28, 9-11. 14. 22; 30, 8-11. 15), which is evidenced by their rulers' reliance on armaments (2, 7; 22, 8-11; 30, 15) and political alliances (2, 22; 28, 15; 30, 1-7; 31, 1-3).

Unlike Amos, Isaiah allows more room for hope. He stresses the notion of the remnant (7, 3; 8, 18; 37, 31-32), whose characteristics are holiness (4, 3), faith (10, 20-21) and justice (28, 5-6), and he proclaims the coming of the Messiah (11, 1-9; 9, 1-6). But Isaiah, too, sees the announcement of the impending day primarily as a summons to conversion, faith and justice.

In the 7th century B.C., in Judah, Zephaniah (1, 14-18) paints a gripping portrait of the Day of Yahweh. It involves a military catastrophe that will punish the nation for the rampant idolatry during the reign of Manasses and Amon. He, too, looks for the salvation of a remnant, whom he describes as humble and lowly (3, 11-13), and he invites the lowly of the earth to seek justice and humility, so that they "may be sheltered on the day of the Lord's anger" (2, 3).

At the beginning of the 6th century B.C., Ezekiel predicts the Day of Yahweh on several occasions (7, 10; 13, 5; 30, 3). He envisions a Babylonian invasion, which he describes in realistic detail (17, 12-21; 21, 23-32), in symbolic acts (4; 5; 12), in parables (16, 35-43; 22, 18-22; 23, 25-30. 32-34; 24, 3-14) and in angelic visions (8—11). A priest and devoted adherent of the Law himself, Ezekiel interprets this chastisement as a punishment for idolatry (6; 8; 16; 20; 22; 23), for profanations of the sabbath (20, 13. 16. 21. 24; 22, 8. 26; 23, 38), for violence and bloodshed (7, 23; 8, 17; 11, 6; 22, 7. 29; 33, 25) and for adultery (22, 11; 33, 26). Anxious to uphold God's justice in this chastisement, he stresses individual responsibility and the salvation of the upright (9, 4-6; 14, 12-20; 18; 33, 10-20), and also the conversion of a remnant (6, 8-10; 12, 16; 20, 37). He also goes beyond the time of chastisement to describe at length the cultic worship of a restored Israel (40—48).

The oracle of Isaiah 13, describing the Day of Yahweh to be visited on Babylon, undoubtedly dates from the 6th century B.C. It foretells the destruction of the tyrannical city by alien armies (13, 2-6. 15-16) and eventually identifies the invaders as the Medes (13, 7). Into this portrait of divine judgment it introduces several cosmic brushstrokes (13, 10. 13) which will have a long history in later oracles (Is. 34, 4; 24, 21-23; Hag. 2, 6. 21; Jl. 2, 10; 3, 3-4; 4, 15; Mk. 13, 24-25).

These oracles undoubtedly express the tieup between man's destiny and the status of the cosmos that had always been maintained in the biblical outlook (from Gn. 3, 17-18 to Rom. 8, 19-23). But in Isaiah 13 they have a more precise meaning. When the prophet says that the light of the sun, moon and stars will be extinguished, he is not talking about the end of the existing cosmos; it will continue to exist above the devastated city (13, 19-22). He is referring to Yahweh's victory over the astral deities of Babylon (even as Ezekiel 32, 7-8 depicts the punishment of Egypt by the darkening of its sun god). The prophet's affirmation deals with the triumph of God the creator over the nature deities of paganism.

The book of Joel, which can be dated around 400 B.C., is taken up completely with the Day of Yahweh (1, 15; 2. 1. 11; 3, 4; 4, 14). It distinguishes two occurrences as part of that day.[3] The first is an invasion of grasshoppers and locusts (1—2) that has already taken place; he describes it in reportorial terms, intermingling the traditional military and cosmic brushstrokes in the presentation (1, 6; 2, 2-11). He uses this tragedy to urge repentance on the people (2, 12-17), promising an end to the plague if they do repent (2, 18-27).

[3] Cf. J. Bourke, "Le Jour de Yahvé dans Joël," in *Revue Biblique* 66 (1959), pp. 5-31, 191-212.

In the second part of the book, the prophet uses the same images (3, 4; 4, 15) to describe the judgment of Yahweh on all the nations that have oppressed his people. He announces the gift of the Spirit to the faithful (3, 1-2) and the survival of a remnant in Jerusalem (3, 5) in a paradisiacal setting (4, 18). The first Day of Yahweh is seen as a preparation for, and promise of, the second Day of Yahweh; the latter will bring salvation to his people.[4]

Thus, throughout the prophetic tradition, the Day of Yahweh is God's intervention in history to pass judgment on his people and on the nations. Faithful to his covenant, his promise and his justice, he is going to reestablish due order by chastising the unfaithful and saving the upright remnant; the latter group is mentioned by all the prophets who talk about the upcoming day.

In presenting their depiction of this event, the prophets often indicate that they see it being effected by a catastrophe in history (e.g., a military invasion or a natural plague). They sometimes intertwine cosmic images (e.g., clouds or the darkening of celestial lights), but the meaning of these phenomena is more literary than literal, and they became conventional symbols in the judgment theme.

For the prophets the essential point is to proclaim God's mastery over history and his imminent appearance in glory; his appearance requires that people be converted if they wish to be part of the remnant and to enjoy the salvation he will give to his faithful ones.

Judgment in the Apocalypse of Daniel

The book of Daniel presents the last and most complete proclamation of divine judgment in the Old Testament. Because it inaugurates a new genre in biblical writing (apocalypses) and because it greatly influenced Jesus, it deserves special study.

[4] The other references to the day in the prophets are Isaiah 34, 8 and Obadiah 15 (day of vengeance against Edom), and Malachi 3, 23 (sending of Elias to prepare Israel for the day).

The book of Daniel presents several pictures of the final days. Sometimes it uses imagery (2: the dream of the statue; 7: the vision of the Son of Man), and on one occasion it presents a straightforward prophecy at the end of an historical vision (10—12).

To interpret Daniel's images, we would do well to start with the latter vision, for it presents data that can be tied up with the history of that epoch. The section starts out by relating, in prophetic form, the history of pagan rulers over Palestine since the exile: the Persians (11, 2-4); the successors of Alexander in Egypt and Syria (11, 5-20); in particular, Antiochus IV, who reigned over Syria from 175 to 164 B.C. (11, 21-45). Antiochus' war with Ptolemy VI (11, 25-29), the intervention of the Romans (11, 30), Antiochus' attacks on the temple and his persecution of the Jews—all these things are reported with precision (11, 31-39).

When it describes the final end of the impious king, however, the vision abandons the recital of known historical facts (11, 40-45). It relates his end to the transcendent events at the end of time: the great tribulation and the intervention of Michael, the head of the heavenly hosts (12, 1); the resurrection of many dead people to eternal life or everlasting horror (12, 2-3).

This oracle is the first clear affirmation of the resurrection of the dead to appear in Israel. (Isaiah 26, 19 is too brief, too full of imagery, to allow for a sure interpretation.) Daniel's oracle depicts the resurrection as a prelude to the judgment that will end persecution by Antiochus. The persecutors and apostates (11, 32. 39) will be punished forever; the faithful, particularly the martyred wise men (11, 33. 35), will rise to obtain eternal life.

Thus the resurrection is presented as the means by which Yahweh's judgment will be extended even to the dead on his day. The oracle leaves much obscure, to be sure. It does not say whether this resurrection applies to all mankind. In short, it alludes to divine judgment, chastisement and reward, but it does not describe them in detail. Daniel wishes only to affirm God's triumph at the end of the persecutions and his transcendent judgment on men even beyond the grave.

The vision of the beasts and the Son of Man (7) presents a similar tableau in symbolic form. The symbols are interpreted for the prophet by angels (6, 16-27). The beasts are pagan kingdoms (7, 17. 24), clearly the ones that have exercised power over Israel since Nebuchadnezzar (note the interpretation of the parallel vision of the statue in 2, 31-43). The fourth beast is the kingdom of Syria, represented in particular by Antiochus IV, the persecutor (7, 8. 19-25; cf. 11, 21-45). As in Daniel 11, 45 and 12, 1, Antiochus IV is felled by a divine intervention that constitutes the final judgment (7, 9-11. 22. 26).

Salvation is described in terms of the Son of Man: power over all the nations of the world is entrusted to him (7, 13-14). His title indicates that he is the man par excellence, true humanity as opposed to the pagan kingdoms symbolized by the beasts. Three times Daniel explains that he represents "the holy people of the Most High" (7, 18. 22. 27). After undergoing persecution, the Son of Man receives eternal dominion over all the nations of the earth. Resurrection is not mentioned here, but it seems implied in the fact that the holy ones are first subjected to persecution.

The portrait of judgment in Daniel extends and surpasses all preceding predictions about the Day of Yahweh. As in the earlier prophets, it takes place in history, but it also marks the end of history, because it is a judgment that affects the dead and thus is situated in a new world. Here eschatology is transcendent.

The Meaning of Judgment in the Old Testament

Even our brief survey so far suggests the variety of eschatological representations in the Old Testament. This variety is due to the individual personality of each prophet, to the diversity of their materials and their literary genres, and to the progress of revelation itself (i.e., from the historical judgment of Amos and Isaiah to the transcendent judgment of Daniel).

All the more striking, then, is the constant element that runs through these diverse depictions of eschatology:

1. The sober nature of these portraits of the future. They are painted with a few brief images, as if to respect the mysteriousness of God's future intervention.

2. Certitude about an imminent intervention that will reestablish justice and provide salvation.

3. This certainty is rooted in the sacred history of Israel, in God's election, covenant and promises that already find a guarantee in his past interventions into the nation's history.

4. These prophetic proclamations about the future always seek to inspire faith, conversion and hope. Right now the people must turn to God, and the eschatological oracles attempt to stress the acute urgency of this decisive step. The imminent nature of the events described is a by-product of this sense of urgency. Israel never lost sight of this, because it never abandoned this hope, even though the Lord's Day was put off time and again.

II

THE MESSAGE OF JESUS

Jesus utilized most of the eschatological themes to be found in the Old Testament and Judaism. If we put them into our logical classifications, we can point to several in particular: the great tribulation, the resurrection, the coming of the Son of Man, the judgment, eternal fire, life eternal and the kingdom of God. We shall first examine these varied announcements of judgment, and then analyze the vast fresco of his eschatological discourse.

Announcements of Judgment

These announcements, which occupy a considerable place in the preaching of Jesus, take different forms. We find: simple sentences about the judgment of individuals (Mt. 7, 2. 22-23; 12, 36; 23, 33) or of groups (Mt. 11, 21-24; 12, 39-42; 23, 34-

39; Lk. 19, 42-44); statements about condemnation (Mt. 5, 22; 10, 15. 33; Mk. 12, 40) or reward (Mt. 6, 4. 6. 18; 10, 32; Lk. 14, 14); varied parables which draw their images from human tribunals (Mt. 5, 25-26; Lk. 18, 1-8), from accounting procedure (Mt. 18, 22-35; 25, 14-30; Lk. 16, 1-9), from workmen's compensation (Mt. 20, 1-6), from harvesting (Mt. 13, 24-30. 36-43) and from fishing techniques (Mt. 13, 47-50).

Only in Matthew 25, 31-46 does Jesus give a detailed portrait of this judgment. Several traits indicate that the text underwent elaboration in the literary tradition. The central figure is sometimes called the Son of Man (25, 31), and sometimes the king (25, 34. 40). The judgment affects all the nations of the world, and hence the pagans also, but the reference to helping "the least of my brethren" (25, 40. 45) suggests that the text was applied to a judgment on the members of the Church (cf. Mt. 12, 46-50; 28, 10).

Several authors have conjectured that Matthew constructed the scene from various talks of Jesus.[5] It is not an impossible hypothesis, but it would be risky to try to separate the primitive elements from the later accretions with perfect precision. In any case the principal traits of this scene, and the eschatological elements in particular, find close parallels in the most well attested *logia* of Jesus; thus they can be regarded as faithful expressions of his own thought. Matthew's fresco, then, provides an integrated picture of elements that are scattered about in the various gospels.

The scene opens with the Son of Man coming in glory (25, 31). In talking about the final judgment, Jesus applied this trait of Daniel 7, 13-14 to himself on several occasions (Mk. 8, 38; 13, 26; 14, 62; Mt. 10, 23; 16, 28; 19, 28; Lk. 12, 8; 17, 22-30; 18, 8). Here he presents himself as the judge, while in Matthew 10, 32-33 and Mark 8, 39 he plays the role of a witness before God's tribunal; yet even here he is merely carrying out the ver-

[5] Notably J. A. T. Robinson, "The Parable of the Sheep and the Goats," in *New Testament Studies* II (1956), pp. 225-37; reprinted in *Twelve N.T. Studies* (London, 1962), pp. 76-93.

dict of his Father (25, 34. 41). The angels accompanying him are court assistants, as they are in several other *logia* (Mk. 8, 38; 13, 27; Mt. 13, 39. 41. 49; Lk. 12, 8-9) and in Daniel 7, 10. 16.

The gathering of all the nations for the judgment (25, 32) fits in with the universalist outlook of Jesus (Mt. 8, 11-12; 10, 18; 28, 19; Mk. 13, 10). The separation of the good and the wicked is the fundamental theme to be found in the traditional eschatology concerning the judgment. Jesus alluded to it time and again: note the parables of the weeds and the fish net (Mt. 13, 24-30. 47-50), the parables of the virgins and the talents (Mt. 25, 1-30), his remarks about the coming of the Gentiles (Mt. 8, 11-12), his instructions to the missionaries (Lk. 10, 9. 11) and his admonitions to bear witness to him (Mt. 10, 32-33).

The most original note in this particular tableau is the motif injected into the separation of the good from the wicked. In his other pronouncements about the judgment, Jesus ties it in with men's faith in the mission (Mt. 10, 15; 11, 20-24; 12, 41-42; 23, 37-39) or their witness to him (Mt. 10, 32-33; Mk. 13, 13); he also mentions fraternal charity (Mt. 5, 21-22; 6, 4. 14-15; 7, 1-2; 18, 35; Lk. 14, 14). The novel element in Matthew 25 is that love for "the least of my brethren" is interpreted as love for Jesus himself.

Is it possible that this line of thought is meant to reestablish justification by good works? There are several arguments militating against such an interpretation. To begin with, we must remember that the teaching of Jesus was not organized in systematic form. His emphasis on the importance of charity here does not mitigate his summons to belief and acceptance of the Gospel. Moreover, we must not forget that charity is described here as service rendered to Jesus in the person of his brothers; it is an action permeated by faith, not pure philanthropy.[6]

---

[6] The text does not spell out how this theological charity is possible for pagans who have not heard the Gospel message. This is one of the arguments put forward by those critics who maintain that Matthew reworked this text with the Church in mind. But perhaps Jesus himself saw fraternal generosity as a step leading toward the acceptance of his mystery.

The difference between the basis of judgment in the Old Testament and the basis here reveals the novelty of the scene. In the Old Testament man was always judged on the basis of his conduct toward God: his uprightness, his fidelity to the covenant and his adherence to the law that spells out its demands. Here, however, man is judged on the basis of his attitude toward Jesus. Jesus is the test man faces, the cornerstone that crushes the unbeliever and saves the believer (Lk. 20, 17-18; cf. 2, 34).

The consequences of the judgment are spelled out in terms that were familiar in Judaism and common in the Gospel. The wicked will endure everlasting judgment (25, 46; cf. Dn. 12, 2) and everlasting fire (25, 41; cf. Mt. 18, 8; Mk. 9, 43. 48). The blessed will enjoy the kingdom (25, 34) and everlasting life (25, 46; cf. Dn. 12, 2; Mk. 10, 30).

On the whole, the Matthaean tableau puts the finishing touches on Old Testament revelation about the judgment. It reiterates the essential themes: God will intervene to fulfill his plan of justice and grace; the definitive People of God will be established, and they will receive life and salvation. The Old Testament had already glimpsed the universalism of judgment in Yahweh's day against the nations, and Daniel had opened up the idea of another kind of life—eternal life. The distinctive element in Jesus' portrait of judgment is his own role. He makes himself the central figure in the judgment event; man must accept him to fulfill the will of God. With the addition of this element, the traditional theme attains its fullest development.

The Eschatological Discourse (Mk. 13, 5-27)

This discourse is the product of a major literary effort, as is evident from the differences in the parallel texts of the three Synoptic gospels and from the presence of several of its elements in Matthew 10, 17-22 and Luke 17, 22-37. Several exegetes have even felt that its apocalyptic genre excluded attribution to Jesus, that it had to derive from some Judaic or Judeo-Christian source.[7]

[7] The different hypotheses on the origin of the eschatological discourse are presented in G. R. Beasley-Murray, *Jesus and the Future* (London,

The latter opinion hardly seems probable to me. Why? Because Jesus freely uses the literary genres in vogue among his
contemporaries. Because he often employs the eschatological
themes of the apocalypses in his *logia*. Because the thought of
this discourse accords well with that of his own message. Above
all, because this discourse modifies the traditional perspective of
the apocalypses with a touch of originality that one might well
regard as the mark of Jesus' own thought.

Here we shall consider the elements that are common to the
three Synoptic accounts, because they are more likely to derive
from the earliest stage of tradition. However, we shall leave aside
Mark 13, 9-13 and the parallel section in the other Synoptic
gospels because it seems to fit better in Matthew 10, 17-22. It
may well have been added to the eschatological discourse in
Luke as a commentary on the section that follows (Mk. 13, 14-
20).

The first section of this discourse (Mk. 13, 5-8, particularly vv.
7-8) presents the hallmarks of the *eschaton* that are found in all
the Jewish apocalypses: wars, rumors of war, earthquakes,
famines, etc. But while the Jewish apocalypses sought to date the
eschaton on the basis of these signs, Jesus refuses to hazard an
exact date: "The end is not yet. . . . These things are the beginning of sorrows" (13, 7-8). The day and hour of the end is in the
Father's hands, and Jesus does not try to predict it (Mk. 13,
32).

For Jesus, the authentic augury of the *eschaton* is the ordeal to
be endured by the People of God (Mk. 13, 14-20). He describes
it with the help of two themes from the book of Daniel: (1) the
abomination of desolation (Dn. 9, 27; 11, 31; 12, 11)— a mysterious theme that must at least refer to the person of the antichrist in Mark's mind (cf. 2 Th. 2, 3-4); (2) the great tribulation (Dn. 12, 1). For Jesus, this ordeal is the true sign of the
advent of salvation; the wars and the other classic apocalyptic
signs are not. He cherished this notion dearly: his disciples could

---

1954). On the present status of the question, see J. Lambrecht, *Die
Redaktion der Markus-Apokalypse* (Rome, 1967).

only share his glory by sharing his passion (Mk. 10, 38), by taking up their cross and following him (Mk. 8, 34-35) and by braving the world's hatred (Mt. 10, 17-39).

Salvation itself is the coming of the Son of Man (Mk. 13, 24-27). It opens with the traditional heavenly signs that are presented in Old Testament depictions of the judgment. Verses 24-25 of Mark pick up Isaiah 13, 10 and 34, 4. The literary origin of these elements indicates that Jesus did not intend to provide information about the cosmic aspect of this judgment. For him, the essential point is his coming in glory (Mk. 13, 26), which he describes in the words of Daniel 7, 13-14 (Aramaic text).

If Jesus often applies this text to himself, as we noted above, he does so to announce the glory he will assume after the lowliness of his present condition. He also does it to indicate that he sees himself as the representative of the "saints of the Most High", of the People of God as a whole; it is he who ensures salvation to all men.

Jesus describes his role on the last day in a single phrase: he will gather his elect from the four winds (Mk. 13, 27). It is quite remarkable that he says nothing here about the resurrection, the judgment, the happiness of the just or the punishment of the wicked, even though these are familiar themes in his message. Since a traditional apocalypse would not have failed to mention them, Jesus' silence must be accounted for in terms of his own outlook. He mentions all these themes elsewhere, but when he thinks about his glorious coming on the last day, he is primarily interested in the gathering of his own, in their salvation and in the definitive fulfillment of his Father's kingdom. Therein lies the culmination of his whole mission.[8]

Jesus' View of the Judgment

To depict the judgment, Jesus utilizes themes provided by the Old Testament and Judaic tradition: the resurrection, the coming of the Son of Man, the separation of the good from the

[8] This point has been stressed by E. Lohmeyer, *Das Evangelium des Markus* (Göttingen, [13]1954), pp. 279, 285-86, and by G. R. Beasley-Murray, *A Commentary on Mark Thirteen* (London, 1957), p. 90.

wicked, the fire of Gehenna and everlasting life in the kingdom of God. But he also passes over some of the traditional images: salvation localized on Sion (Is. 54; 60; 2, 1-5; Zech. 14, 16-21); Israel's political sovereignty over the other nations (Is. 60, 10-16; Dn. 7, 14. 27); the temporal prosperity of the salvation era (Hos. 2, 23; Is. 29, 17; 32, 15; 60, 16-17; Hag. 2, 7-8). Thus Jesus clearly underlines the essentially religious character of salvation.

In describing the eschatological events, Jesus refuses to fix their date (13, 32) or to specify the number of the elect (Lk. 13, 23-24). Like all the prophets, however, he depicts it as an imminent happening. Today is the day to decide in favor of Jesus, to take a stand on his mission. John presents Jesus' thought well when his gospel records Jesus as saying that judgment depends on man's decision for or against him (Jn. 3, 18-19; 5, 24). The most novel element in his message is the statement that judgment is embodied in the person of the Son of Man.

Throughout both Testaments, the Bible proclaims that history has meaning, that it is moving toward an encounter with God, and that God's judgment will definitively establish his holy people. The various depictions of the judgment are not meant to describe it so much as to summon men to a conversion in faith. Then, in Jesus Christ, they will receive the wondrous and mysterious salvation that God offers them.

Peter Müller-Goldkuhle/*Oberhausen, West Germany*

Post-Biblical Developments in Eschatological Thought

I

ESCHATOLOGY IN THE EARLY CHURCH

1. *Delay in the Parousia and Development of Church Structures*

In the later documents of the New Testament it is evident that interest in the practical life of the Christian community had already become a major concern among the second generation of Christians. This trend intensified in the post-biblical period. The delay in the parousia had not yet become a conscious problem, but efforts to cope with it were already being made in the day-to-day life of the Church.

Christians now were forced to prepare for a longer stay in this world. Cultic rituals, pastoral epistles and catalogues of virtues and vices bear literary witness to this reorientation. Belief in an imminent parousia remained very much alive, but the fact of organizational growth led to a shift in interest, and the eschatological side of Christian faith suffered its first diminution.

More and more this shift in emphasis became a doctrinal problem. Didn't the growing institutionalization of ecclesial life represent a betrayal of Christian eschatological expectation, and hence a desertion from the apostolic heritage? The first phase of ecclesial activity had gone on almost unconsciously, but now people became consciously aware of the tension between escha-

24

tological expectation and organizational development in the Church.

Several reasons explain why this tension did not develop into an acute crisis of belief. First of all, rabid belief in an imminent parousia, excluding all possibility of Church organization and all interest in day-to-day life, was a rarity from the start; people became aware of the problem gradually rather than being confronted with it all at once. Second, the Christian people had an outlook that was permeated with what Bultmann has called "sacramentalism": [1] in short, they were convinced that the powers of the world beyond were already operative in this world within the sacramental life of the Church. Third, there developed a reasoned apologetics accounting for the delay in the parousia. Expectation of an imminent parousia was an authentic element of apostolic tradition, to be sure, but it had to be related to other authentic elements of that tradition, such as the sacraments and offices in the Church.

The growing moralizing tendency shifted the emphasis from the nearness of the parousia to its suddenness, and it stressed the threat of imminent retribution. The delay in the parousia was attributed to the mercy of God, who was offering man one final chance at conversion.[2] Christ's resurrection was offered as proof that, despite the delay, the promise of parousia and general resurrection would be fulfilled. The only acute crisis that developed from this tension between parousia and Church was Montanism, which may well be regarded as a reaction of older prophetism and eschatological belief against the growing trend toward institutionalization.

The following age could not brook this tension in Christian eschatology. It found relief in the breakup of eschatology into two extremes of the spectrum: strict emphasis on the here and now at one end, and strict emphasis on the distant future at the other end.

[1] Cf. R. Bultmann, *Geschichte und Eschatologie* (Tübingen, ²1964).
[2] The fading of eschatological expectations went hand in hand with the evolution of the sacrament of penance.

The present-day connotations of eschatological pronouncements were now stressed. The Church herself, as an institutional-
ized cultic community, already participated in the world beyond.
The rise of a Christian empire under Constantine and Theodo-
sius greatly influenced many Church Fathers, persuading them
that the promised *eschaton* was already embodied in it.[3]

Everything that could not be explained in terms of the present
was projected into the distant future. The events which had once
been expected in the near future—parousia, resurrection, judgment and the new creation—now were expected in the distant
future. In this way the eschatological tension of the apostolic era
was neutralized. Considerable speculation about the world to
come persisted, but the note of passionate longing for it was
muted.

2. *The Kingdom of God*

Even in the theology of St. Paul, the notion of God's dominion
had begun to fade into the background. Now, in the era of the
early Church Fathers, it was recast completely, becoming directly involved in the process of resolving eschatological tensions.

To be sure, we still find significant chunks of the older eschatology in the texts; essentially, however, the kingdom of God was
projected into the distant future as a transcendent reality to
come. The kingdom of God became the state of blessed repose
and peace that was to be the reward of the righteous. Christ
created the preliminary requisites, and the era of the Church was
the ultimate preliminary stage, but neither was driven toward
this goal by an inner dynamism. Only the second coming of
Christ would usher in the kingdom of God.[4]

From the apocalyptic literature of late Judaism and the influence of hellenistic cosmology, another line of thought on the
kingdom took shape. It viewed the kingdom as something im-
manent in history and present here and now. The kingdom of

---

[3] For example: Lactantius, Eusebius, Augustinus and Caesarius of
Arles.

[4] Cf. O. Koch, *Eigenart und Bedtutung der Eschatologie im theologischen Aufriss des ersten Clemensbriefes* (Bonn, 1964).

God rested on the order of creation, and it was realized in the course of history. The establishment of an imperial Church and the christianization of the whole empire realized the definitive form of the kingdom willed by God.

Augustine's notion of the kingdom incorporates these two lines of thought. On the one hand, the city of God is the future, definitive shape of Church and State together; it will give heavenly bliss to redeemed individuals. On the other hand, he equates the visible form of the Catholic Church in history with this city of God.

Augustine himself, to be sure, managed to transcend this outlook by spiritualizing both concepts and thus recovering the older eschatology. The *civitas Dei*—the invisible community of the predestined elect—has already dawned in the visible Church; it grows toward its fulfillment in a process of constant struggle with the equally invisible *civitas terrena*. Visible, concrete history is merely the reflection of this invisible process. After Augustine, this eschatological notion of the kingdom was lost once again, while the notion of the kingdom as the hierarchical Church maintained its force.[5]

3. *The Individual and the Eschaton*

When the broader eschatological perspectives became blurred, the eschatological expectations of the individual took on greater significance; under the influence of hellenistic thought, an extremely individualistic focus took over. The fate of the individual soul became the center of attention, and men pondered the soul's life after death, blissful immortality, personal judgment, the various states of the soul after death, and happiness in paradise. Early Christian art on tombstones testifies to the profound influence of platonic thought on the Christian outlook.

This shift to an individualistic emphasis was reinforced by the fact that individual eschatology abetted the growing stress on moralism. In the East, under the influence of gnosticism, stress

[5] Cf. A. Wachtel, *Beiträge zur Geschichtstheologie des Aurelius Augustinus* (Bonn, 1960).

was placed on the soul's progressive ascent through purification, training and sanctification. In the West, under the influence of Judaic and Stoic thought, the notion of retribution took the foreground. The *eschata* were projected wholly into the future, as reward or punishment for behavior in this life.

A third characteristic was a danger posed by hellenism. Christian eschatology was in danger of being overly spiritualized by hellenistic ideas. The realism of traditional Christian thought was constantly challenged by the platonic *sōma-sēma* notion, by the belief in spiritual enlightenment through *gnosis,* and by the Manichaean longing to free the soul from matter so that it might return to its lost homeland.[6]

4. *Time and History in Greek and Christian Thought*

The delay in the parousia also led the Church to ponder the nature of history and, specifically, the relationship between world history and salvation history. This necessarily led to a conflict with pagan antiquity's understanding of time.

It was Origen who made the one major attempt to resolve the conflict. He sought to incorporate biblical salvation history into a cyclic, metaphysical, supratemporal cosmology derived from gnosticism and neo-platonism. He sought to identify the latter's movement of descent and ascent with the Christian saga of sin and redemption. He intermingled the here and the hereafter, immanence and transcendence, creation and redemption, historicity and eternity; the result was a watering-down of Christian doctrine.

The repeatability of the salvation process tended to relativize the salvific work of Christ, and this was probably the main reason for the Church's adverse reaction. The *apokatastasis* itself, however, could be given a thoroughly Christian interpretation, and we find this in the works of Gregory of Nyssa and Irenaeus.[7]

---

[6] Reacting against gnosticism, Irenaeus painted a very clear and sensual portrait of the *eschata,* giving major stress to the resurrection of the body.

[7] Cf. G. Müller, "Origenes und die Apokatastasis," in *Theologische Zeitschrift* 14 (1958), pp. 174-90.

The problem is seen most clearly in the work of Augustine. Here the unhistorical view of neo-platonism runs head on into the biblical interpretation of history. To depict the Bible's linear view of time, Augustine uses various categories that are familiar to his contemporaries: *ante legem—sub lege—sub gratia;* the seven ages of the world; the four world empires. To this he adds the neo-platonic view of God, with its qualities of immutability and timelessness.

The sinful fall toppled mankind "from the a-temporal heights of paradise into the historical realm of damnation and longing for a new creation".[8] In Christ and his Church, the supra-temporal realm of a transcendent God becomes operative in this world; the process becomes visible in the conflict between the two kingdoms that takes place in history. When the re-created cosmos attains its definitive form, however, it will no longer be subject to change and alteration.

This view preserved the unity of world history and salvation history without invoking a cyclic notion of time. However, the eschatological aspects of salvation within time were lost in the process; the "last things" were projected beyond time.

5. *The Thousand-Year Kingdom*

Chiliasm presented its own special problems. We find only a few allusions to it in the New Testament (Apoc. 20), but it is clearly evident in the apocalyptic literature of late Judaism. From there it made its way into Eastern and Western Christianity during the era of the Church Fathers. During periods of suffering and persecution, people were especially receptive to the comforting notion of such a kingdom and looked forward eagerly to it. The concept had a steady stream of opponents and defenders, and there were widely divergent interpretations of the "millennium".

Slowly and imperceptibly the notion of chiliasm faded as the imperial Church took shape. Augustine gave a new interpreta-

[8] A. Wachtel, *op cit.,* p. 43. We do not find a unified treatment of eschatology in Augustine's works. The eschatological themes vary with the subject being treated.

tion to it, situating the thousand-year kingdom in this world and depicting it as the interim period between the incarnation and the parousia. Interest in eschatology and apocalypse had faded.[9]

II
ESCHATOLOGY IN THE MIDDLE AGES

1. A Frozen Concept of the Church

Augustine's many-faceted notion of the *civitas* survived in the Middle Ages in a radically diminished form. The kingdom of God was identified with the visible Church. His notion of the *civitas* was fused with the political concept of the Roman empire: the whole earth would live quietly under the *pax Romana*. The notion of the Church bore the imprint of this outlook.

The empire of the Christian West was the kingdom of Christ. Its immutability seemed to be assured by Daniel's prophecies about the four earthly kingdoms. Only the parousia, coming some day in the future, would terminate the whole process. The present lacked all eschatological dynamism; growth and development could only take place spatially, insofar as the empire extended its rule over additional peoples.

The elaboration of Canon Law led to new developments in the process of institutionalization. The notion of the Church was cast in juridical terms. The Church was the *societas perfecta,* the Christian body corporate; the doctrine of the two swords, divid-

---

[9] Only later did the old notion surface again in the reform movements of medieval and modern times; it fell prey to secularization in the thought of the rationalists. Cf. *Dict. Théol. Cath.* 10, pp. 1760-63. "There seems to be no justification for saying that the approach of the year 1000 produced great anxiety in the Western world over the end of the world, the antichrist or imminent judgment. There were eschatological warnings here and there, to be sure, but they were around both before and after the turn of the millennium. To some extent they were concomitants of the transition taking place in the West, a transition that became more visible every day, but they did not have any far-reaching impact": F. Kempf, *Die mittelalterliche Kirche* I (Freiburg, 1966), p. 398, footnote.

ing power between Church and State, held sway. The Church became "the mirror image of cosmic order and the sacramental embodiment of God's redemptive theocracy".[10] Living in this conceptual framework, Anselm of Havelberg (d. 1158) asked how the evident mutability of the Church could be reconciled with the immutability of God.[11]

2. Eschatology and Apocalypse in Popular Piety

The Middle Ages bore witness to an ever widening chasm between clergy and people, between theology and popular piety, and between educated higher clerics and uneducated lower clerics. This paved the way for the development of various currents of thought that were tied up with each other in a variety of ways.

The old thrust of Christian eschatology, for example, took on new life. It showed up in various guises as a reaction against the official concept of the Church. In the 12th century and the first half of the 13th century, a widespread eschatological piety dominated Western Christianity—for the last time, apparently.

A variety of popular movements gained ground, imbued with specifically eschatological notions or embodying stifled ideas. They intermingled Christian and non-Christian ideas, and they were often related to one another. All of them were characterized by the rough intensity of the medieval spirit.

Here we encounter the apocalyptic notions of the Crusades and the Flagellants, the heretical movements of the Albigensians, Waldensians and Hussites, the movements for reform and uprisings of the poor, the widespread response to Joachim of Fiore and Savonarola, and the recurrent vitality of fanatical apocalypticism in times of war and catastrophe. The medieval outlook found expression in crusades, miracle stories and mystical visions, in mystery plays, paintings and literary works, in the well-

---

[10] *Evangelisches Kirchenlexikon* 3, p. 561.
[11] Cf. W. Kamlah, *Apokalypse und Geschichtstheologie: Die mittelalterliche Auslegung der Apokalypse vor Joachim von Fiore* (Berlin, 1935).

ing tide of membership in the strict monastic orders, in numerous new institutions and charitable works, in the fanciful portraits of wandering preachers, and in the development of the funeral liturgy.

Besides the prolific depictions of heaven, hell and purgatory, the second coming of Christ was a major theme. The end of the world and the general judgment were vividly portrayed, while the antichrist was personified in the changing events of history. The *Dies irae,* which may well date from the turn of the 12th century, gives us a glimpse of the ideas that characterized contemporary popular piety: individual salvation or damnation, fear and trembling before the judgment, punishment or reward for one's deeds with the resultant stress on justification by works and ethical conversion. This may well explain why that age was later designated as the "Dark Ages".

The person and activity of a Francis of Assisi must be viewed in terms of this popular eschatology rather than in terms of socio-ethical ideals. His poverty betokened the eschatological behavior of the Christian and proved the authenticity of his preaching about the imminent end. It represented full-blown imitation of Christ, who was ready to appear; Christ's coming was the news that Francis had to proclaim.[12]

3. *The Theology of History*

Despite the obstacles mentioned above, the problem of history was not dropped in the Middle Ages. Augustine's portrait of a universal world history was the framework within which men explored the meaning of history. They found its meaning in the *providentia Dei,* God's eternal plan for the world. The events of each succeeding era unfolded under the watchful eyes of God.

The events of history embodied the recurrent struggle between God and his enemies, between Christ and antichrist. The conflict would reach its glorious climax in the great judgment that lay

---

[12] Cf. N. Wicki, *Die Lehre von der himmlischen Seligkeit in der mittelalterlichen Scholastik von Petrus Lombardus bis Thomas von Aquin* (Freiburg-Switzerland, 1954); R. Petry, "Medieval Eschatology and St. Francis of Assisi," in *Church History* 9 (1940), pp. 54-69.

around the corner. In describing this unfolding process, authors utilized the seven-stage classification inherited from the patristic age (starting with the apostles' preaching to the Jews and ending with the final epoch of the judgment itself), or else they expropriated Augustine's version of chiliasm, which depicted the era between incarnation and parousia—i.e., the era of Church history—as the kingdom.[13]

The work of Joachim of Fiore (d. 1202) must also be examined against this backdrop of dynamic apocalypticism and the medieval view of history. His lush allegorical treatment sought to provide the definitive historical interpretation of the apocalypse, explaining papacy, imperial power and the historical events of the day.

Joachim divided history into three ages: the age of the Father, the age of the Son and the age of the Holy Spirit. This division was not simply an updated version of Montanism; it also represented an important stage in the secularization of eschatology.[14] The year 1260 was to mark an historical climax in the process, inaugurating the third and final phase. It would be the era of the monk, the Johannine era, when the beatitudes would be preached, the Jews converted, the war and schism ended.

To be sure, this multi-stage depiction did relativize the unique salvific activity of Christ. Yet Joachim did manage to recapture something of the dynamism of classical Christian eschatology, because he did not present the various eras as sharply compartmentalized stages. He did not see one era ending and another beginning in a neat linear progression. The power of the awaited "Church of the Spirit" was already at work now, slowly and painstakingly eating away at the clerical, imperial Church and transforming it into a spiritual Church. The climactic year in the process would be 1260.

The other great eschatological perspective in the Middle Ages developed within a christology oriented around salvation history. It was first elaborated by Rupert von Deutz (d. 1135) and his

---

[13] Cf. the great work of Rupert von Deutz on the theology of history, *De victoria Verbi Dei* (Migne: *P.L.* 170, 703-804.

[14] Cf. W. Kamlah, *op. cit.*

theological view of history. "In his view, the whole of creation (both the visible and invisible world) was created for the God-Man Christ. Christ would gather up all creation under his headship and, as the royal high priest, would offer it to the Father in a cosmic liturgy." [15]

This view survived with Albertus Magnus (d. 1280) and Duns Scotus (d. 1308). It also survived in scholasticism as part of the question concerning the *causae incarnationis,* but here its significance was greatly reduced, and confined to academic circles.

4. *Eschatology in Theology and the Magisterium*

The chasm created between popular piety and university theology enabled scholarly views on eschatology to lead an isolated life of their own. As yet there was no systematic treatment of eschatology. Various remarks on eschatology were put together, depending on the *quaestio* under consideration.

The first compilations of *Sententiae* in early scholasticism also represent the first attempts to provide a systematic eschatology. Peter Lombard (d. 1160) incorporated his tract on eschatology into the total system of scholastic theology, and this became the accepted procedure in subsequent *Sententiae.*[16] In the hundred years between Peter Lombard and Thomas Aquinas, the basic cast of eschatology was firmly established.

The introduction of Aristotelian thought in the latter half of the 12th century was significant for eschatology in two respects. To begin with, the prevailing anthropology, derived from neoplatonism and augustinianism, had viewed the soul as the real man. Now William of Auxerre (d. ca. 1235) presented the soul as the *forma corporis.* Soul and body were now seen as two coequal constituents of human nature. As a result, the resurrection of the dead was almost turned into a basic postulate of natural philosophy.

[15] Cf. W. Kahles, *Geschichte als Liturgie: Die Geschichtstheologie des Rupertus von Deutz* (Münster, 1960).

[16] A singular exception is the *Sententiae* of Gandolph of Bologna (d. ca. 1190).

Moreover, the clash between various university faculties forced theology to fashion proofs so that it could vindicate its standing as a scholarly science. It was thus induced to adopt the natural-science methodology of Aristotle, with its emphasis on substance, accidents and various causes. This trend involved the danger of overschematization and of an excessively atomistic outlook. The danger was even greater in eschatology, where there was less dogmatic certainty and less conceptual clarity. While there was much room for the play of conceptual fantasy, the cohesiveness and overall meaning of eschatology was lost.

The nature of the beatific vision became the main question in scholastic eschatology. Sharply divergent opinions arose because of the stress on individual happiness, the varying opinions on the primacy of the will or the intellect, and the differing allegiances to platonic or aristotelian epistemology.

Yet, despite this, some remnants of Christian eschatology survived. The glory of the beatific vision was regarded as the culmination of grace, and grace was viewed as the beginning of the beatific vision. Thus the simultaneous juxtaposition of the *eschaton* and the here-and-now was restored to theology. Unfortunately, this insight was buried in the tract on grace, while eschatology was supposed to deal mainly with wholly future events.

Medieval pronouncements by the magisterium conformed to the general pattern described above. Disputes arose over the fate of the individual in eschatology and over purgatory, limbo and the beatific vision. The question of man's interim state between death and the general resurrection kept alive the problem of general eschatology. It was a doctrine to be believed, but interest focused on individual eschatology. The pronouncement of Benedict XII, in his Bull *Benedictus Deus* (1336), froze the issue and left it unresolved until our own day. The Bull *Laetentur Coeli* (1439) basically recapitulated the conceptions of an earlier day on this question.[17]

[17] The eschatology in the Supplement of the *Summa Theologica* of St. Thomas Aquinas cannot be regarded as his work even indirectly. On the whole question, see N. Wicki, *op. cit.*

5. The Mystics

Medieval mysticism posed its own distinctive eschatological problem. Did the blessedness of mystical encounter with God belong to the realm of faith or to the realm of actual vision? Was it a question of eschatological longing or a real anticipation of the beatific vision? The texts of the mystics themselves seemed to allow ample room for either interpretation. Most likely, the answer to this question must be sought in scholastic theology's treatment of the relationship between grace and the beatific vision. We cannot expect the mystics to clarify the issue for us.[18]

III
ESCHATOLOGY IN MODERN TIMES

1. Eschatology in the Overall History of Ideas

The unity and teleology of history remained the basic considerations in modern man's attempt to understand history. The interpretation of these items, however, took on many different shapes, and a growing trend toward secularization became evident.

An eschatology oriented around salvation history had already been undermined in the patristic age; in the Middle Ages it was replaced by a view of history founded on divine providence. Now the Renaissance revolutionized the whole emphasis. It was man, not God or his eternal plan, that gave meaning to history. Man was the one who gave unity and impetus to history.

Even the efforts of men like Pascal, Bossuet and Vico could not stem the new tide of thought. Rationalism and enlightenment philosophy developed a view of history based on temporal progress and man's ethical life in the human community. Man was traveling on an ascending path, moving toward ever fuller stages of human perfection.

[18] Cf. B. Weiss, *Die Heilsgeschichte bei Meister Eckhart* (Mainz, 1965).

The idealistic philosophies of Fichte, Schelling and Hegel viewed history as the foreordained unfolding of the Absolute, or as the return of the whole process to its starting point. But the impact of these ideas was short-lived, and they ultimately provided fuel for the next stage of secularization in positivism and materialism.

Anti-rationalist thinkers like Kierkegaard, Schopenhauer and Nietzsche and the philosophers of history in our own century were washed away by the tide of total secularization. The meaning of history was no longer posed as a question; the belief in man's steady progress continued in unreserved positivism, to which even Marxism fell prey.[19]

2. Eschatology in the Church

The popular apocalypticism of the Middle Ages gradually faded away in the post-tridentine era. The counter-reformation cast of theology, the new trends in popular piety, the torpidity of eschatological ideas and the modern trends in the history of ideas contributed to this process.

Dogmatic theology maintained the drift of medieval eschatology, allowing the distortions mentioned above to surface all the more. The tracts became more and more academic. Hairsplitting questions were piled one atop the other. The content of classical theology continued to be watered down, and there was no authentic eschatological outlook.

The first break in this pattern occurred in the German-speaking world during the Enlightenment, when theologians energetically freed themselves from scholastic concepts and methodology. Eschatology came sharply into the foreground because of the anthropocentric outlook of the Enlightenment, its emphasis on individual happiness, humanism and moralism, its concept of progress and its rediscovery of the notion of the kingdom. But even though the new treatises seemed to differ sharply from those

[19] Cf. K. L. Löwith, *Weltgeschichte und Heilsgeschehen* (Stuttgart, 1953).

of late scholasticism, they did not provide any significant elaboration of eschatology.

Substantive reassessments of eschatology occurred first within the romantic stream of the Catholic restoration. Against the backdrop of idealistic philosophy, the Tübingen school of theologians rediscovered the unity of history, its dynamism and its eschatological overtones within the framework of salvation history.

Leading the way was Franz Anton Staudenmaier (d. 1856). On the basis of his discussions with Hegel, he undertook a new exploration into the theology of history. His work stressed the unity of all history in the real immanence of the divine Spirit and its dialectical development in the play of conflicting forces. He unified world history and salvation history on the one hand, and salvation history and the history of revelation on the other hand; he also took account of the inner eschatological thrust in each period of history.

Staudenmaier managed to recapture the old tension that had pervaded Christian eschatology, the tension between God's already completed salvific work and the culmination still to come. This approach enabled him to rework the standard dogmatic tract on eschatology as well. He elaborated it in terms of death, resurrection and judgment, clearly pointing up the salvific character of the *eschaton*. Special stress was given to the christocentric nature of eschatological salvation and to the imperfect but real presence of the *eschaton* here and now. It was a major attempt to unify individual eschatology and general eschatology. This era of renewed interest in the theology of history came to an abrupt end, impeding the diffusion of these ideas.[20]

By the middle of the century, neo-scholasticism had cast aside the theology of the romantic school. The old strands of scholastic theology, which had been shredded in the German school, were resolutely mended and taken up once again. The earlier escha-

[20] Cf. P. Müller-Goldkuhle, *Die Eschatologie in der Dogmatik des 19 Jahrhunderts* (Essen, 1966).

tology, with all its weaknesses, was embraced once more. Lacking any real insight into history, it stressed moralism and tended to become more and more atomistic. The authentic meaning of Christian eschatology was completely lost in it. With good reason it has been called a "physics of the last things".[21]

One notable exception to this trend was Matthias Josef Scheeben (d. 1888) and his incarnational theology. Grace and glory as man's incipient and ultimate participation in the salvific reality of the incarnation formed the great eschatological perspective of his work, which he termed a "theology of glorification". He treated it from a suprahistorical, metaphysical viewpoint rather than from the viewpoint of salvation history. But his treatment preserved the tension in Christian eschatology and the religious nucleus of Christian faith far better than the speculations of his contemporaries managed to do.[22]

Neo-scholastic dogmatic treatises on eschatology remained in this rather pitiable state until after World War II. Only since then have we seen a slow shift in outlook. Historical and exegetical criticism of the Bible, encounters with eschatological ideas in Protestant circles, and the challenge posed to older ways of thinking by science, philosophy and exegesis have led to a reappraisal of eschatology in the Catholic world. The result has been to raise many questions about the older eschatology of neo-scholasticism and to make clear the need for a complete reformulation.[23]

[21] Cf. Y. Congar, "Fins derniers," in *Rev. Sc. Ph. Th.* 33 (1949), pp. 463-84.

[22] Cf. P. Müller-Goldkuhle, *op. cit.* Eschatology does not seem to have borne fruit in the French or Anglo-American sector either. Only the debate over the possible mitigation of punishment in hell kept eschatology alive as a topic within the Church. The same topic was to be considered by Vatican Council I, along with the notion of the particular judgment, but eschatology never came up for consideration.

[23] Two pioneers in this new effort were Gottleib Söhngen in Germany, who sought to dialogue with Karl Barth and Emil Brunner, and Jean Daniélou in France, who tackled the work of Oscar Cullmann. Cf. J. Ratzinger, "Heilsgeschichte und Eschatologie," in *Theologie im Wandel* edited by Ratzinger and Neumann (Munich, 1967), pp. 68-89.

3. *Eschatology in Protestant Theology*

In contrast with the sterility of medieval eschatology, the Protestant reformers found their way back to authentic Christian notions about the *eschaton*. Martin Luther stressed the notion *simul iustus et peccator* in his study of justification, ecclesiology and government. His emphasis on this notion and on present anticipation of the *eschaton* in Word and sacrament restored the old tension in Christian eschatology.[24]

In his comprehensive theology of the kingdom, John Calvin depicts the eschatological thrust imbedded in all temporal embodiments of the kingdom. Concrete forms of Church, State and society are oriented toward the transcendent fulfillment of all creation. These authentically Christian insights subsequently fell prey to the secularizing thrust of rationalist thought. Focus was shifted to the progress and advancement of human society within time.

Martin Luther also continued the line of medieval apocalypticism. He gave historical shape to the battle between Christ and the antichrist, preaching the imminence of the last day and the threat of God's judgment on the world. This tradition was continued by burgeoning radical sects during the reformation period, by chiliastic apocalypticism during the Thirty Years War, by large segments of the pietistic movement, by the refugee communities of the post-napoleonic era, and by other modern sects that interpret time in such a manner. The more official theology neglected eschatology, the more it was emphasized by other circles.

At the turn of the present century, a new emphasis on eschatology appeared in Protestant theology. Johannes Weiss and Albert Schweitzer revived the old problem about the delay in the parousia, which had already been noted by Reimarus. The problem was discussed at great length; at the same time Karl Barth was casting theology in an eschatological framework, and Rudolf

---

[24] Cf. U. Asendorf, *Eschatologie bei Luther* (Göttingen, 1967).

Bultmann was reshaping theological methodology in existential terms. All this has resulted in the new eschatological awareness of the present day. Encounters with modern science and new philosophical approaches have stimulated further questions about this subject.[25]

[25] Cf. W. Ölsner, *Die Entwicklung der Eschatologie von Schleiermacher bis zur Gegenwart* (Gütersloh, 1929).

Edward Schillebeeckx, O.P./*Nijmegen, Netherlands*

The Interpretation
of Eschatology

The Christian believes that the living God showed the uniqueness and power of his unconditional love for man in Jesus Christ, and thus revealed himself as man's salvation. The first Christian generations confessed this ineffable event and expressed this confession in many varied ways in the books of the New Testament. These books therefore give us interpretations of the Jesus-event against the background of the Old Testament sphere of understanding.

The dialectic of the development of dogma or tradition shows that, in order to be faithful to this original event, the Church was constantly obliged to give a fresh interpretation of this apostolic interpretation. This problem became acute for the first time when Christianity with its Palestinian culture and corresponding interpretation was transplanted to an environment with a Hellenistic culture and mentality. The New Testament still shows clear traces of the difficulties experienced in this "translation".

1. We listen to this message now, in our own age. And this means that in our different situation and our different sphere of understanding we react to this Christian message with constant questioning. Therefore, the relevance of the message concerning the "ultimate things", the *eschata,* or the final and definitive salvation of man, implies the need to analyze our own sphere of understanding, not only from the point of view of the sociology and

philosophy of our own culture, but also theologically. But, precisely because our modern self-understanding carries our whole past with it, we cannot understand our present mental outlook if we do not take equal care to understand our own past. To try to understand and assimilate the eschatological message of the Bible today without a critical understanding of what theology made of it in the many centuries of its past with a constantly changing mental outlook would be wholly inadequate. And a first glance at this process already makes it clear that the constantly renewed assimilation of the Christian message is connected with the changing views on man and the world, as they live in common thinking and are formulated by a succession of philosophical schools. To examine the differences in outlook that succeeded each other in the Church's 2,000-year-old tradition is therefore a hermeneutical requirement in the interpretation of the Christian confession of the *eschata*.

But this same investigation must penetrate into the depths of the Old and New Testament origins of this eschatological confession. This process shows that different cultures clash with each other and inspire different kinds of questions. It also shows that, while becoming aware of all these differences, the believer is really trying to interpret and reflect on the meaning of that phase in history in which he himself lives. The Old Testament is then seen as the key source for the explanation of the life and death of a people who become aware of being God's people, just as the New Testament became the literary key source for the explanation of Jesus' life and death. Therefore, both the Old and New Testaments already have an *interpretative* function: they are "hermeneutics in action". But for us this collection of writings itself becomes again something that is in need of interpretation. And so hermeneutics becomes the interpretation of an interpretation.

Although the problem of interpretation is thus itself already one of the facts of the Bible, it has become more acute today than ever before, and this for two main reasons. First, we no longer belong to the same culture; we no longer have the same mentality or the same outlook on man and the world, as those that prevailed in the days when the original and the later interpretations of the Christ-event were formulated. The distance in time makes our problem far more difficult. The culture of the Semites and that of Hellenism at least had in common the fact that they were both part of "antiquity". Yet a modern translation is possible because the ancient self-understanding of man is one of the elements that has shaped our modern self-understanding. Pluralism is never radical. Although there is no identity, there are always channels of communication between the various interpretations. Second, we belong to an age which acknowledges the demands of textual and historical criticism, an age which considers it immoral to surrender oneself unconditionally to something without some rational justification: all people, including those of good will, reject *a priori* a kind of blind faith which has no human and genuine intelligible basis. Even with our unconditional obedience of faith we can no longer avoid the need to make the eschatological dogmas intelligible and in some way understandable. Today faith simply demands that the believer pass through the ordeal of a new interpretation of his faith if he wishes to be faithful to the message of the Gospel.

It is impossible to spell out the rules for this new way of thinking about eschatology in an abstract and formal manner within the limited scope of this article.[1] I limit myself therefore to giving the result of a personal investigation which may show how in fact our eschatological belief took shape in the interpretation of biblical history. This embodies a great deal of hermeneutical matter in a concrete way. My approach starts from modern interest in man's earthly future, one of the key points in man's self-understanding today.

2. Today we observe a basic shift in the way man looks at history. The more or less explicit identification of history with the past which dominated the writing of history since the beginning

[1] Among Catholics an attempt was made by Karl Rahner, "Theologische Prinzipien der Hermeneutik eschatologischer Aussagen," in *Schriften zur Theologie* IV (Einsiedeln/Zurich/Cologne), pp. 401-28.

of its modern phase is now yielding to a view which sees history more as events in the making, events in the process of arrival, and therefore as happenings in which we ourselves play an active part.[2] The "future" is of primary importance in what we call "history". And so the concept of "man's earthly future" begins to exercise a kind of polarity in man's thought and knowledge, while in the past—at least in the West—the future dimension of history was almost considered only as a matter of the *finis ultimus,* the ultimate end of man, beyond and after this earthly life.

Since the rediscovery of man's true historicity as a creature of "time" that on the basis of its past sets its course of life in the present toward a future, eschatology is seen as a *question* which lies embodied in man's existence. Man's experience does not simply run on in time, with an undercurrent of "becoming"; it also implies an element of time-consciousness. This does not allow him to escape from time, but it allows him in a certain sense to transcend the lived time, although he cannot put this time-transcending permanence into words, at least not positively. This time-consciousness which makes man reach beyond experienced time into both the past and the future makes man's questioning about the "beginning" and the "end" particularly relevant. It therefore seems to me that to inquire after the future is an "existential" in our human condition. Although caught up in time and never outside it, man is not the prisoner of time in his historical growth; he transcends time from within. That is why he can never feel satisfied. Within this time-condition man is therefore free to achieve a certain *openness* with regard to time. He can do so because he can also indulge like an epicure in the short-lived joys of the temporary condition in which he lives. But if he takes this time-consciousness seriously, he cannot avoid facing the question of the meaning of human history. For every moment of his free existence implies present, past and future. His

---

[2] Cf., among others, R. Wittram, *Zukunft in der Geschichte* (Göttingen, 1966); G. Ebeling, "Die Welt als Geschichte," in *Mensch und Kosmos* (Zurich/Stuttgart, 1960), pp. 103-14; G. Greshake, *Historie wird Geschichte* (Essen, 1963); J. B. Metz, *Zur Theologie der Welt* (Mainz/Munich, 1968).

freedom indeed is exercised in the present but only insofar as this present sets its course toward the future. The pure present is always on the point of sliding into the past. Man's future-building freedom thus essentially presupposes an "open" eschatology, an expectation of the future, a will toward the future which, in itself, slips into the ambiguity of all history-making freedom.

3. When in our old culture, mainly concerned with the past, we thought and spoke about God's transcendence, we almost naturally projected God into the past. Eternity was something like an immobilized or immortalized "past"—"*in the beginning was God*". Of course we knew quite well that God's eternity embraced man's present and man's future, that God was both first and last, and as such also a Present that transcended our human present. On this point the older theology developed marvelous insights which have by no means lost their relevance. In a culture which constantly looked toward the past there obviously existed a powerful mutual attraction between "transcendence" and eternity on the one hand and an immortalized "past" on the other. Today, however, our culture is firmly turned toward the future as something that our culture itself must build. And so the Christian notion of "transcendence", supple and capable of more than one meaning, has to go through the same process. The meaning of "transcendence" therefore comes closer to what in our time-bound condition we call "future". If divine transcendence transcends and embraces man's past, present and future *from within,* the believer will preferably and rightly link God's transcendence with the future as soon as man has recognized the primacy of the future in our time-bound condition. And so he will link God with the future of man, and, since man is a communal person, with the future of mankind as a whole. When we once accept the reality of a genuine belief in the invisible reality of God who is the true source of our understanding of God from within this world, this new understanding of his transcendence will lead to the new image of God in our new culture.

In this cultural context the God of the believer will manifest himself as "he who comes", the God who is our future. This implies a far-reaching change: he, whom we formerly saw as the "wholly Other" in our old outlook on man and the world, is now seen as the "wholly New", he who is *our future* and who creates anew man's future. He shows himself as the God who gives us in Jesus Christ the opportunity to build the future, to make all things new and to rise above our own sinful history and that of all mankind. Thus the new culture becomes an inspiration to rediscover as a surprise the Good News of the Old and the New Testaments, the Good News that the God of promise has put us on the way to the promised land, a land which, like Israel of old, we ourselves must claim and cultivate, trusting in his promise.

4. In order to avoid too hasty conclusions, one should not lose sight of the biblical basis of what I have called this new understanding of God. The new culture is but an occasion and stimulus to rediscover the living God as "our future" in the Old and the New Testaments. But according to the Bible the basis of the eschatological expectation of the future is the certainty, in faith, of an actual relationship with God. This actual relationship with the God of the covenant, which makes the past present again, must not be sacrificed to the primacy of the future. As T. Vriezen, the well-known Old Testament scholar, correctly stated: "The expectation of the future lies in the certainty of the belief in the actual relationship with God." [8] The basis of our *hope* is therefore our *faith* in Yahweh who reveals himself in both past and present as the living God of the community.

This is understandable when we realize that the present and its past are the only basis on which we can build a future; otherwise we simply land ourselves in futuristic fantasies. The past belongs essentially to our human condition which in its present is oriented toward the future. And the interpretation of Old Testament history shows that the past only becomes clearer in the present when again and again it is seen in the light of the future. In the Bible the interpretation of a past event always coincides with the announcement of a new expectation for the future. The

[8] *Hoofdlijnen der theologie van het Oude Testament* (Wageningen, 1966), p. 467.

past is "read again" in a manner which makes it once more actual, and thus it becomes a guarantee for the hope of a new future.[4] Embodied in a canon of Scripture, the traditional material which voices future expectations is raised above the level of its original intent. And in this dimension of its own future the past remains forever actual. The etiological explanation of the present from the past is at the same time a confession that new salvation is dawning.

Thus the critical (form-criticism) analysis of the Old Testament theme of "taking possession of the land" shows that its connection with the theme of "fulfillment and promise" is a theological reflection on the *actual* possession of the "holy land". Here we have therefore a theological view of history arising from actual existence and providing an interpretation of the past as well as a pointer toward the future. If we want to understand Israel's history as a promise, we shall find that this promise is not an absolute starting point without a pre-history, as if it were a kind of Word of God which promised Israel a new future out of the blue and from on high, and drew a picture of it with all its future and observable features. On the contrary, Israel only began to understand its own history as a divine promise when it looked back from its present to its own past and recognized there God's faithfulness, a faithfulness which naturally means an expectation of future salvation to man as he is involved in history and therefore looks toward the future. Looking back, we see Yahweh's faithful-

---

[4] A full critical exposé is impossible here, but the following is an illustration. In the national-religious epos of the book of Joshua we read: "Called and mightily helped by our God, Joshua entered upon the land at the head of the twelve tribes and conquered all of it, after which each tribe was allotted its own territory. Thus God fulfilled all his promises; not one was unfulfilled" (Jos. 21, 45). Here a past (somewhat different here from what actually happened) was reinterpreted, and this interpretation became at the same time an expression of a new belief in national restoration after the Assyrians had destroyed the realm of the ten northern tribes in 721. When, after 650, Assyrian power began to wane, Israel's hope of an untroubled possession of the "whole of Yahweh's land" revived. This book, written under King Josiah (640-609) and recast during the exile, thus describes the past from the angle of a new hope of the future, the signs of which were seen in contemporary events.

ness as *promise;* looking ahead, we see it as an expectation and continuous fulfillment, and on the basis of this faithfulness our expectation constantly opens up a new future through a history which stretches beyond us. It is therefore through the historical development of its tradition that Israel began to understand what was meant by God's promise. Because Israel remembered certain meaningful events from the past and associated them with new events of the present, both past and present illuminated each other, and thus it experienced and interpreted its history as the gradual fulfillment of a divine promise. Within this concept of history the present itself was seen as a new promise, a new door opening to a new future. And ultimately the whole earthly history becomes the unfolding of an eschatological expectation.

It is therefore a *lived tradition,* a history of the transmission of traditions, which underlies the Israelite's interpretation of history as a divine promise, as God's saving activity, as covenant, and, implied in all this, as revelation. An event experienced by the community is handed down to future generations only insofar as, and because, it has a special meaning for that community. And the community discovers the meaning of this event because it has passed through a particular history which carries traditions and insights with it. Therefore, the past event only reaches us with the meaning it had for that community and never without it or outside it. The history of the transmission of traditions thus reveals the gradual unfolding of the meaning of the event to future generations with all the additions and corrections which the constant reading and rereading of the event has brought to it in the further development of history. We can only discover the meaning of a past event for us *now* by also taking into account the history of traditions without arbitrary interpretations. And so we see here the principle of hermeneutics. Only when we understand history as a critically examined history of traditions can we understand it as a promise as it was lived in Israel and received its first definitive fulfillment in Jesus Christ.[5]

[5] This shows that the schema of "promise and fulfillment", as developed, for instance, by J. Moltmann (*Theologie der Hoffnung,* Munich,

If we see "biblical history" as an event handed down to us in a believing and critical interpretation, we can also see that the reference to the future is contained in the present of the People of God as it lives within the context of this history of traditions. "Future" is an intrinsic dimension of the present, related to what must still happen in time without allowing us to see its future shape at present. This biblical structure of the prophecy of the future which sets the present within a living history of traditions rejects on the one hand any "de-eschatologization" of time (there is no room for a radical "eschatology of the present") and on the other hand demands a rejection of all apocalyptic elements from the expectation of the future (apocalyptic thought thinks from the future to the present).

Because of man's essential historicity, future means a future starting from the present and therefore from the past. Although its actual shape remains hidden, the future is an intrinsic element in man's self-understanding. This hidden reality is therefore intrinsically related to the actuality. This has been insufficiently understood by J. Moltmann.[6] In this sense there can be no true eschatology of the future without a certain eschatology of the present. Although the future has an element of "not yet" in it, we cannot neglect the element of "already". In fact, only the "already" allows us to say anything meaningful about the still unknown future. It is therefore typical that the Old Testament never describes the unknown future in totally new and unexpected terms. Hope always looks for some ideal "restoration", the particular features of which are supposed to be known from the past. The total picture, however, is always new. Expectation is not looking for a simple re-edition of the past. Israel hoped for the fulfillment

---

1965), can only be understood if we presuppose a conception of history as the "history of the transmission of traditions", as elaborated by W. Pannenberg in his many works, particularly since he has abandoned this schema of "promise and fulfillment" in order to put more weight on the continuity of the history of traditions. See *Theology as History* (Vol. 3 of *New Frontiers in Theology*, New York, Evanston and London, 1967), pp. 252ff., with nn. 60, 61 and 69.

[6] Cf. W. Kreck, *Die Zukunft des Gekommenen* (Munich, ²1966), p. 207.

of what Yahweh had already done in its desire for the total achievement of it all. The reactualization of the past in the present with an eye on the future makes Israel expect with increasing tension that future which only Yahweh can bring, and which then will be definitive, once for all. Such an expectation has nothing to do with crystal-gazing or an unveiling of the future. It is rather an insight of faith, gained by the knowledge of God's dealings with his people. Only the unconditional surrender to Yahweh's faithfulness and the living traditions that are related to it can bring any certainty about the future. In terms of man's historicity Yahweh's faithfulness is expectation of a future certainty about the goodness of the plan of creation which is both the beginning and the *eschaton*, the ultimate end. It is *tôb me'od*, "very good" (Gen. 1, 31). In other words, man's future, as seen by God (the Bible puts these words into Yahweh's mouth), is "very good", a future of salvation. The lack of salvation, temporary or possibly final, is of man's own doing. It is interesting here that biblical thought about the beginning ("protology") is intertwined with eschatological thought. This "protology", as formulated in the final draft of the creation story in Genesis, can only be understood on the basis of actual experience of God's faithfulness with its consequent eschatological expectations. The story of creation is therefore also an eschatological statement.

5. What, however, is the connection between the future and the *eschaton?* O. Procksch, G. von Rad and T. Vriezen [7] rightly maintain against V. Maag [8] that in the Old Testament the belief in God's dominion is not identical with the kingdom of God in the eschatological sense. Moreover, for centuries Israel practiced its religion without expecting a hereafter. Apart from the very late (mainly the last two centuries before Christ) apocalyptic eschatology in the Old Testament, expressions such as "the latter days" (*acharit, eschaton, be'acharit hajjamin*—in the last days;

[7] O. Procksch, *Theologie des Alten Testaments* (Gütersloh, 1950), p. 591; G. von Rad, "Basileia," in *Theol. Wört. z. N.T.* I, pp. 566f.; T. Vriezen, *Hoofdlijnen, loc. cit.*

[8] V. Maag, "Malkût Jhwh," in *Supplements to Vetus Test.* 7 (1960), pp. 129-53.

cf. Is. 2, 2) [9] do not refer to an existence beyond this earth, beyond history, but to a future within this world. The *eschaton* is marked by "newness" and "universalism", but it is all in a concept of history which remains on this side of the beyond. To this Ezekiel and Deutero-Isaiah add the idea of an approaching "nearness". Throughout the prophetic tradition the picture of God's day of judgment is reflected on the screen of earthly history; it is the picture of an expectation of a future in this world, this history. Only in Daniel and the very latest apocalyptic insertions into earlier prophetic traditions does the "Day of Yahweh" put a full stop to history. The *eschaton* then refers to a situation beyond this earth, or at least to the time immediately preceding the end of time. But even in the probably late apocalyptic passage in Isaiah 24—27 the last days are still seen within the reality of the history of this world: the old People of God is then given its final eschatological status without mentioning whether history will still go on after that. Not until the book of Daniel is there a question of a transcendent eschatology or talk of a post-historical existence, expressed in the powerful religious symbol of "resurrection". That there will be a future for the historical past, and even for the dead, appears only very late in the Old Testament.

For centuries, therefore, the belief in Yahweh could be practiced meaningfully without the assertion of a transcendent, post-historical and final fulfillment. This development in revelation shows that one does not live religiously *for the sake of* the hereafter. The development of Israel's faith shows that the unquestionable value of the covenant, the actual relationship between the historic Israel and God, provides the hermeneutical context for a belief in a transcendent eschatology. The "setting in life" of the eschatological expectation beyond this world is the temporal all-surpassing meaning of the actual relationship with the living God. This conceals the hidden urge toward a transcendent future. For some time devout Israelites had already had some inkling of

[9] See also Gen. 49, 1; Num. 24, 14; Deut. 4, 30; Jer. 23, 20; 30, 24; 48, 47; 49, 39; Ez. 38, 16; Dan. 10, 14; Hos. 3, 5; Mich. 4, 1.

THE INTERPRETATION OF ESCHATOLOGY

the idea that even death has no power over him whom God loves. Most powerfully perhaps in Psalms 16, 49, and 73, the spiritual experience of relationship with God is expressed which would sooner or later destroy the idea of the *sheol* (the state after death as one of excommunication from life—i.e., from life in this world with one's fellows in communion with God), and so pave the way for a transcendent eschatology. In these Psalms Yahweh's faithfulness fosters the idea that love must be immortal and definitive, that through this love we know that we are "in God's hand" not only *in* but also *after* death. Beyond this vague hunch the psalmists had no appropriate terminology to express the existential certainty of this spiritual experience and the concept of resurrection that marked the first suitable formula.

The present, then, understood as the actual relationship with God and experienced historically as God's dealings with man, is not only the hermeneutical principle for the interpretation of religious expectations of the future but also the principle which links the future of this earth with the transcendent *eschaton*. The Bible gives us no anticipating historical report over this *eschaton*. We know nothing about the transcendent ultimate things— judgment, Christ's return, heaven, hell, purgatory—*except* insofar as they are already indicated in the course of historical events expressing the actual relationship between the God of the covenant and mankind, particularly in Christ, "the last Adam" —i.e., "the man of the *eschaton*" (1 Cor. 15, 45; cf. Apoc. 1, 18; 22, 13).

Therefore, eschatology does not allow us to withdraw from earthly history because only in the depth of this history can eternity begin to take shape. The post-terrestrial *eschaton* is but a question of the manner in which what is already growing in the history of this world will receive its final fulfillment. This analysis seems to confirm Rahner's position: "To speak from the present to the future is eschatology; to speak from the future to the present is apocalyptic." [10] Eschatology is the expression of the belief that history is in God's hands, that the history of the world

[10] *Op cit.* (n. 1), p. 150.

can reach its fulfillment in communion with God and that it
will be brought to this fulfillment in Christ who embodies God's
promise. Eschatology does not allow us to "cash in" on the hereafter but it is a task to be achieved responsibly by all the faithful
within the framework of our terrestrial history. Faced with the
real evil existing in history, eschatology expresses the belief that
the true faithful can and must bend this history into the salvation
of all. This must be done within the perspective of present world
history, in "newness" and in the context of universality. This
salvation must be achieved now in our history, in this world, and
so this history becomes itself a *prophecy* of the final and transcendent *eschaton*. It is the promise of a "new world", a powerful
symbol which sets us thinking and above all acting. And the
credibility of this promise lies in the actual renewal, now, of our
human history. Through their "justification" the faithful themselves become responsible for the "newness" of this human world
whose dimension in depth will be perpetuated into eternity. For
this eternity does not come after our time or our history but is
both the transcendent and the intrinsic ultimate fulfillment of this
history itself.

All exegetes accept that the biblical words about the kingdom
of God are connected with Jesus' own message. In Jesus the
world is given the last promise. But in Jesus of Nazareth we see
that the *eschaton* is a post-historical *event* about which we can
only speak from the angle of a history understood in the terms of
faith. The raising of Jesus to the status of Lord is a saving act of
God which, at one point, turned the history which ended in his
death into a *fulfilled* history. That is why it touches our own
terrestrial history. We are faced here with a real event which is
embedded in history and yet is not historical but eschatological.
While the apocalyptic approach puts the *eschaton* at the end of
the history of this world, Christianity has put it within history
itself. Because of the ambiguity of human freedom this history
remains open to the future; on the other hand, it already carries
the judgment within it. For in the man Jesus the future of man-

kind has been revealed to us: the fulfillment of the life of Jesus himself, in both its individual and collective social aspects.

The "new world", in Jesus Christ irrevocably promised and actually on its way, is therefore not a prefabricated reality but is coming into being as an historical world within the historical process of acting-in-faith in this world. In its present realization this history is a prophetic pointer to the final fulfillment which can no longer be achieved or expressed in terms of terrestrial history. It does not "end" this terrestrial history by leaving it behind but by bringing it wholly to its fulfillment. That is why we can only speak haltingly about the final eschatological kingdom and mainly in images and symbols that have grown out of the "contrast experiences" (the "this-situation-should-be-changed" type) in our still growing world: "There shall be neither mourning nor crying nor pain any more" (Apoc. 21, 4); ". . . new heavens and a new earth in which righteousness dwells" (2 Pet. 3, 13). In the concrete the hermeneutics and exegesis of the final kingdom therefore consists mainly in the stressing of the actual commitment of the faithful to the *renewal* of this human history of ours. Only this constructive Christian activity provides a credible exegesis or interpretation of what we believe when, as the People of God, we confess: "I believe in eternal life." In other words, I believe in an earthly, historical life that is truly *Life* and that is stronger than death for him who believes in the living God who gave man the final promise of his faithfulness in Jesus Christ "forever and ever" and to the end of time.

The fact that transcendent eschatology arose very late in the history of revelation defends genuine religion against Freudian or Marxist criticism which maintains that belief in the hereafter is by definition projection and alienation. The joy of being able to serve Yahweh has made the believer in God's revelation keep silent about the hereafter for centuries in spite of the pressure of opinions that were current in neighboring cultures. Israel's greatest tragedy was that it had to make up its mind about its ideas of death—in other words, about the experience of the fact that death still snatched this living-with-God away from God's sovereignty.[11] But in the end, this living-with-the-living-God on this earth had to yield its secret: such a life makes even death a relative event; it is stronger than death.

There is no trace of a natural immortality of the soul in either the Old or the New Testaments. But we *do* find there the primacy of the actual covenant relationship with the living God who is faithfulness and therefore also "future", even for the faithful one who has died. The kingdom of Yahweh cannot be reconciled with "being dead". In its cultural and religious history Israel had already passed its peak before it realized—in fact, only two centuries before Jesus came—the genuine eschatological implications of its old faith and saw that history, seen as the dealings of God with man through his covenant, contained far more than could be related in a purely historical fashion. In its historicity, history is a prophecy which points beyond the historical events to the transcendent *eschaton*. This means that only an analysis of the way the Christian lives in this world can tell us something in very sober terms about the great eschatological themes, resurrection, judgment, the parousia, the fulfillment of a bodily mankind in full communion with God—in short, about what we call "heaven", a reality which only man himself can twist into a negation, a self-built hell, the rejection of that love which is the foundation of this total communion.

On the basis of these few hermeneutical principles, *theology* can be seen as the rational and meaningful unfolding of that which shows itself in history. It is not the *only* possible rational interpretation of reality, but it can show that in its affirmation of reality the Christian faith gives a humanly meaningful, intelligible and responsible interpretation of man and his world. Thus it can enter into a genuine dialogue with the many other interpretations current in this world—for the good of all.

[11] Cf. the key text, Deut. 30, 19-20. See also G. Schunack, *Das hermeneutische Problem des Todes im Horizont von Römer 5 untersucht* (Tübingen, 1967), p. 54.

Enrico Castelli Gattinara di Zubiena/*Rome, Italy*

The Time of the Incarnation
and the Time of Secularity

The problematic of de-mythologizing is based on an equivocation: the unity of time—or better, on the non-distinction between the time of the *historia rerum gestarum* and *sacred history*.

The time of *sacred history* is *sui generis;* the other is *time lost.* Time lost is that of the past, the present and the future, but especially of the *past,* when we speak of history, since the *present* is not presentable, and the *future* is aleatory.

One history is of the past; the other, that of the future, is a *science.* For example, the biological history of an organism is that which determines what will occur (based on what has occurred) since the cycle of vitality involves the elements A, B, C, etc. in a succession which becomes the history (future) of that development—that is, the history of what can be anticipated (the time of secularity).

1. There is a *sacred history* and a *history of the sacred.* The two histories coincide only on one point: sacred history is also the history of the sacred, but the history of the sacred can be something other than sacred history, as it is presented in Christianity.

2. The non-coincidence of sacred history with the history of the sacred is the index of a history of the anti-sacred, from the viewpoint of Christianity. Would a history of the secular be possible? The question allows a twofold distinction: (a) the secular

as opposed to the sacred from the viewpoint of the secular; (b) the secular as opposed to the sacred from the viewpoint of the sacred. The two viewpoints do not coincide; indeed, from the viewpoint of the sacred there is only one sphere, and the secular is an aspect of sacrality; from the secular viewpoint, the sacred is what stands opposite to it. Hence, we can answer the question by saying that there are two histories of the secular. To go from one to the other means to confuse everything, to go astray.

3. To go astray is one of the aspects of human existence. The histories of the sacred and of the secular agree on this, but they do so in a different way: those of the sacred recognize a *status naturae lapsae,* and those of the secular recognize the *fact,* speak of temptation, but do not speak of a first temptation.

4. To speak of temptation signifies speaking of attractions (it does not signify speaking of an origin, a *primum*). Human nature is attracted to . . . (or tends toward . . .). That it is sick is a fact, verified by the secular histories of the secular, but we cannot speak of lost health. The signs are lacking (one of the aspects of the going astray).

The historian of the secular—in the face of the definition of history that one of Shakespeare's characters terms "a tale told by an idiot"—cannot take sides because he says he does not know if the definition is true or false. There thus arises the problem of the significance (and insignificance) of *tale* and *idiot.*

5. What is to be understood by *sign?* Kierkegaard writes: "A sign is the negation of immediacy, or a second state of being, differing from the first. It is not thereby affirmed that the sign is not something immediate, but that what it is as a sign is not immediate—in other words, that as a sign it is not the immediate thing it is. A nautical mark is a sign. Immediately it is a post, a light or some such thing, but it is not a sign immediately; that it is a sign is something different from what it immediately is. The failure to observe this distinction lies at the bottom of all the mystifications caused by "signs"; for a sign is a sign only for one who knows that it is a sign, and in the strictest sense only for one

who knows what it signifies; for everyone else the sign is only what it immediately is. Even in case no one had erected this or that as a sign, and there was no understanding with anybody that it was to be regarded as such, yet when I see something striking and call it a sign, it is qualified as such by reflection. The striking trait is the immediate, but that I regard it as a sign (a reflective act, producing something out of myself) expresses my conception that it must signify something, but the fact that it must *signify* something means that it is something else than that which it immediately is. So I am not denying the immediacy of the thing when I regard it as a sign without knowing definitely that it is a sign or what it should signify." [1]

6. The problem of significance (which is the same problem of the *sign*) runs over into sacred and secular history. The following is an example:

[1] Kierkegaard adds: "A *'sign of contradiction'* is a sign which contains in itself a contradiction. . . . A sign is not what it immediately is, for no sign is immediately a sign, since 'sign' is a qualification of reflection. A sign of contradiction is one which draws attention to itself, and then, when attention is fixed upon it, shows that it contains a contradiction. And in the Scripture the God-Man is called a sign of contradiction—but what contradiction might there be in the speculative unity of God and man in general? No, in that there is no contradiction; but the contradiction, the greatest possible, the qualitative contradiction, is that between being God and being an individual man. To be a sign is to be, besides what one immediately is, also another thing; to be a sign of contradiction is to be another thing which stands in opposition to what one immediately is. Immediately he is an individual man, just like other men, a lowly insignificant man; but the contradiction is *that he is God.* . . . The God-Man is the sign of contradiction. And why? Because, replies the Scripture, he shall reveal the thoughts of hearts" (S. Kierkegaard, *Training in Christianity* [Princeton, 1964], pp. 124-26).
 "To *believe* in [one's] own destruction is impossible. To understand that, humanly, it is [one's] own destruction, and then nevertheless to believe in the possibility, is what is meant by faith. . . . This is the sound health of faith which resolves contradictions. The contradiction . . . is that, humanly speaking, destruction is certain, and that, nevertheless, there is possibility. Health consists essentially in being able to resolve contradictions. So it is bodily or physically: a draft is indifferently cold and warm, disparate qualities undialectically combined; but a healthy body resolves this contradiction and does not notice the draft. So it is also with faith" (S. Kierkegaard, *The Sickness unto Death* [New York, 1954], pp. 172-73).

The Credo's "suffered under Pontius Pilate" is history. Is it sacred? Is part of the history which is called *sacred,* truly sacred history? This is disputable, because the *significance* of the part is partial, and a partial significance is insufficient—that is, not very significative. The Gospel speaks of Caesar: "Render to Caesar what is Caesar's." This is history in the same way that "Caesar invaded Gaul" is history. The history of the Cyrenian is also history. The fact that it is *sacred cannot be demonstrated* precisely because sacrality is not inherent in the event in and for itself. An event is an event, and nothing more. When it is represented as something else, the problem of its event-aspect arises, and together with it the sense of transcendence (of that which transcends the event, lies outside it, that which is the *beyond,* the *extreme*). But there is no history about what goes *beyond.* A demonstration of this is the following: A triangle is drawn on a sheet of paper and the sum of its angles is shown to be equal to two straight lines. The demonstration proceeds, as is well known, by prolonging one of the sides and having recourse to the postulate of the parallels. Let us say that the demonstration constitutes the event $X - Y$ (that is, that event which was realized on the day X in the year Y). Further study will reveal that it took place on a blackboard having the dimensions Z, and hanging on the wall of a local site in the place W, etc. But the postulate of the parallels transcends the event (is beyond it), lies outside history. Yet there exists a history of geometry (of the beyond of the event, of what transcends it). In what sense does this exist? In the sense that a few men in the year X have *discovered* the relation A, B, C, etc. by using the instruments 1, 2, 3, etc. *To discover* what is beyond the sign (the triangle, the circle, the point, the straight line) does not yet mean to attain the *sacred.* Some have said it means getting closer to it; others have said it means getting further away from it. Getting closer to it, because it means intruding on what is beyond the event (what exceeds time); getting further away from it, because it means getting away from what has speech and a name. It means to intrude on the anonymity of knowledge.

7. Then does a metaphysics of witness exist besides the witness of *what is always present,* that of what is discovered? In order to answer this question, we must distinguish two modes of bearing witness: that of geometry—which bears witness, for example, that if we have a point and a straight line, only one parallel to the straight line can pass through the point; and that of the one who asserts that on a given day, at a definite hour, this so-called postulate of Euclidean geometry was enunciated by a certain person. Thus we have a witness of the discovery of *what is always true* and a witness of someone who in time (a particular time) has discovered something. These two witnessings give rise to two histories: the history of the necessary and that of the contingent. There are two histories because the necessary is discovered in a certain time, as a result of which the discoverer draws a series of propositions in a definite succession. The succession—involving a before and an after—seems to be itself the history; instead, it is only the structure of a relation, while it is certainly history for anyone who endeavors to determine the relation (to understand it).[2] To understand it means to consider

[2] On the subject of time as the means of eliminating the difficulty of assenting to two well-founded but opposed judgments, the observations of Bernardo Varisco deserve consideration: "If time were only the means of eliminating the opposition between two well-founded judgments, there would be an ineradicable arbitrariness in referring one of these to the present and the other to the past which is absolutely unknown. . . . Take, for example, 'the sun is shining' and 'the clouds are hiding the sun'. Certainly, the opposition vanishes when we refer the first to the present and the second to the past, as well as when we refer the second to the present and the first to the past. The arbitrary aspect is undeniable; conversely, it is not absolutely possible to allow arbitrariness here; we always necessarily refer to the present the judgment of the two which is based on a *sensation,* and to the past the one which is based on *memory.* Hence, the difference between memory and sensation possesses an essential importance in this respect; it is not licit to affirm that the judgment based on memory is based on experience in the same way, with the same right, as that based on sensation; if we wish to be understood, we must say in inadequate language that memory signifies precisely a past experience, although it is present as memory. And then the whole expressed interpretation concerning time disappears. . . . Undoubtedly, oppositions arise against our present thought; but never against an experiential foundation, when we do not forget to appreciate the difference between *sensation* and *memory.* They arise even in our

it as pre-existent (outside the process itself)—that is, outside history. But certainly this attribution of a beyond in the act to be understood is not understandable in the way that the relation discovered is understandable. To say that it is paramount is to say little, but it is a *witnessing,* with which history has a meaning and without which history has no significance.[3] The question revolves around the significance. When we say that "it has no significance", we intend to say that "we have lost the connecting thread", or better, that "we cannot get at the source" (origin).

---

rational processes, or more exactly, in the processes directed at the exposition of contemporary laws. Now, in this field there is no example of oppositions that can be eliminated by means of time. Let us take a geometric example. There is a straight line XY and a point A outside this straight line: it could be that no parallel could be drawn through A to XY; or that two parallels could be drawn through A (in the latter case, neither of the straight lines drawn through A, internally to the acute angle formed by the two parallels, could encounter XY without entering into a relation of parallelism with XY). The opposition among the three hypotheses is evident; moreover, the three hypotheses are all equally well founded insofar as a geometry can be constructed on each. It is certainly impossible that the opposition be eliminated by the medium of time; indeed, geometry absolutely excludes time, since it is incapable of being under any aspect the theory of a happening. However, the opposition is eliminated very simply by recognizing that the three hypotheses, and hence the three geometries, are irreconcilable. In short, only one of the three hypotheses can be objectively true. As we see, the affirmation that time is the means for eliminating opposition is unjustified; indeed, it has no value in oppositions of a rational character, while its value in oppositions of an experiential character presupposes time, and therefore is of no use for our understanding" (B. Varisco, *Linee di filosofia* [Rome, 1931], pp. 85-86).

[3] "Time begins with the cessation of the present and ceases with the cessation of this cessation," writes Franz von Baader (*Ueber den Begriff der Zeit*). Time (or better, "history"), continues Baader, is an invention of "merciful love which temporizes with its dispersed children". It is easy to say that the definition has no significance; one could object that it has too much. It enables us to see the path of a sacred history. To such a history the "dispersed children" oppose the cries of Macbeth: "Things bad begun make strong themselves by ill" (Act III); "Nothing is but what is not" (Act I); "Life . . . [signifies] nothing" (Act V) or the indifference of those who have time to listen to the considerations about time, because their history is that of the one who is not obliged to prolong his own existence against the onslaughts of men and things. These represent a conscious and an unconscious version of one and the same method of procedure.

And again: the origin beyond the actual witnessing is an empty way of speaking, something indescribable and unsuitable.

The *beyond* is what is suitable. Is it convincing? Yes, if (in-effable) conditions exist (grace); otherwise, no. Here we have the whole principle of a *sacred history* which is a history *sui generis* but not a *history of the sacred*.

A *sacred history* entails an experience of the sacred (for ex-ample, "the folly of the cross"), and a metaphysics of witnessing that is a metaphysics of the experience of the sacred. However, a *history of the sacred* does not entail such an experience; it is a philosophy which also has its cross: "the cross of folly"; and if we wish to pursue it further, "the cross of the folly of the cross".[4] It is a philosophy of the going astray, because in a certain sense it is a philosophy of the recent past (of that which the present mo-ment records) [5] for which all future is prohibited.

This is a philosophy of the experience of an insuperable soli-tude (one of the aspects of demonization, that of the *eritis sicut dei* of the biblical serpent); of some happening in general for which every consideration of the event-aspect itself is precluded. Those who say "We do not know what demonization signifies" are right. But *to be right* does not suffice *to understand*. They belong to the history of the secular (and to the philosophy of the secular) which is that of secularity for those who are on the other side. Every event is in itself ambiguous, and history is the history of ambiguity. This can be illuminated by a secular phi-

[4] We can also say with Nietzsche that "atheism and a kind of 'second innocence' go together" ("The Genealogy of Morals", in *The Birth of Tragedy and the Genealogy of Morals* [New York, 1956], p. 224), but on condition that we are certain that the situation of uneasiness (the anxiety of some folly) is definitively eliminated by the complete tri-umph of atheism (the deliverance of "mankind altogether from its feel-ing of being indebted to its beginnings, its *causa prima*" (F. Nietzsche, *op. cit.,* p. 224). But we are not certain of such a certainty, even in fol-lowing a philosophy of the secular. There are reasons for concluding that a reflection *sub specie aeternitatis* in terms of a consideration *sub specie temporis* which is not also *sub specie moriae* is a rash procedure —that is, a folly.

[5] The distinction between *memory* and *sensation* has no value for this philosophy, which however does not surmount the objection of Varisco.

losophy (in other words, a philosophy of ambiguity). Such a philosophy is nevertheless *without common meaning*. To answer that "the inquiry must go beyond the common meaning" is to formulate a statement without meaning until the return (after multiple experience) to that *common meaning* which is at the metaphysical basis of every experience, because beyond the common meaning, in this case, lies oblivion (and a loss: oblivion is not an increase). This is oblivion of human nature as it is represented by existence, by continual option: oblivion of the stimulus itself to the question (what is a *sign?*): a secularization.[6] In conclusion, it is a renunciation of *understanding* through an incessant and fruitless reasoning about *understanding*, through arbitrary substitution of the word for *participation*. As I have mentioned more than once, the *common meaning* is the meaning of a twofold danger: the danger (which can become fatal) of an uncontrolled impulse, and the danger of the prevalence of an idea (*status alienationis*).

This is the philosophy of a rash orbit around a closed line (a slow but continuous spiral which advances inexorably toward its dead point); an obstinate refusal to hear, because the distinction between past and present (memory and sensation) is repeated *ad nauseam*, is a *present* distinction. And only a dialectical distinction allows the distinguishing of yesterday from today. This is the

---

[6] Nietzsche's sublime and solemn cry concerning myth is not without significance: " 'The edge of wisdom is turned against the wise man; wisdom is a crime committed on nature': such are the terrible words addressed to us by myth. Yet the Greek poet, like a sunbeam, touches the terrible and austere Memnon's column of myth, which proceeds to give forth Sophoclean melodies" (*The Birth of Tragedy, op. cit.*, pp. 61-62). And the philosopher of Zarathustra adds further: "All that is called evil by the good, must come together in order that truth may be born. . . . *Beside* the bad conscience hath hitherto grown all *knowledge!*" (F. Nietzsche, *Thus Spake Zarathustra* [New York], p. 223) because "not everything may be uttered in presence of day" (*ibid.*, p. 184) and it is "not the height, it is the declivity that is terrible! The declivity, where the gaze shooteth *downwards*, and the hand graspeth *upwards*. There doth the heart become giddy through its double will" (*ibid.*, p. 156). This is an echo in apocalyptic key of Roger Bacon's medieval aphorism: "Libenter enim gustamus de ligno scientiae boni et mali; sed difficiles sumus ad lignum vitae" (*Opus maius*, I, 71).

philosophy of the continual postponement, because *signs* are not definitively *significative* and history really seems to be "a tale told by an idiot", rather than the sacred history of the *kairos* which has its roots in the Pauline dogma of the *pleroma,* which could also be called the "time of the divine incarnation" in the fullness of the resurrection.

Anton Grabner-Haider/*Graz, Austria*

The Biblical Understanding of "Resurrection" and "Glorification"

If the Christian message is to be proclaimed to modern man as a life-giving force, its central precepts will have to be continually re-examined. This process emerges as one of dialogue between the message that is being passed on and those who hear it, a dialogue that explains the Gospel's content while also promoting further discussion of it. Furthermore, it is not simply the hearers who question the Gospel but also vice versa. The Christian message must be open to such encounters and to constant reclarification. Moreover, these encounters should take place in such a way that historically-conditioned man can discover himself in Jesus Christ's historically-conditioned witness of faith.[1] The constant factor in this process of understanding, reapplying and handing on ("tradition") is man, living in history, acting in freedom and personal responsibility, and constituted as a physical and social being.[2]

What then does Christ mean for us today? More precisely, what are we to make of the biblical belief in "resurrection" and "glorification"? What did the biblical writers mean us to understand by these two concepts, and what is their significance for us

[1] Cf. G. Hassenhüttl, *Geschichte und existentiales Denken* (Wiesbaden, 1965), pp. 4f.

[2] Cf. W. Kasper, "Geschichtlichkeit der Dogmen?", in *Stimmen der Zeit* 92 (1967), p. 404; J. Schoiswohl, *Fortschritt in der Kirche* (Graz, 1968), pp. 8ff.

today? How do we proclaim them now in a meaningful way, and what place do they have in our lives? [3] These are the questions I would like to examine briefly in this article in the light of the biblical—particularly the Pauline—understanding of these two concepts. Raising such questions at all presupposes that what the biblical writers intended us to understand by these concepts is by no means self-evident.

I

NEW TESTAMENT ESCHATOLOGY

Belief in resurrection and glorification belongs in the larger area of biblical—more specifically New Testament—eschatology. First, therefore, we have to have at least a basic idea of what New Testament eschatology involves. At this stage in the Church's history it was believed that the world and mankind were heading for a new and imminent future, a future that breaks into the temporal order of world and man. With it will come what is perfect, and it will drive out what is imperfect (1 Cor. 13, 10). This future, which is also the end, is the Lord Jesus Christ (Phil. 4, 5) who, through his resurrection, has become the Lord of all creation. It is he who is awaited and it is he who encompasses the world's duration. Mankind's expectations are centered on him (cf. 1 Thess. 1, 10; 1 Cor. 1, 7; Phil. 3, 20). But the "day" of his coming has already started. Already it has cast its light over God's creation. Even now the "Day of the Lord" is approaching this world, and its proximity makes itself felt. Creation lies in its shadow, and men are already a part of it (1 Thess. 5, 8).

The New Testament sees Christ as the future of the world and of man. What is this future? It is both with us now and yet still removed from us. New Testament eschatology as a whole,

---

[3] H. Schlier, *Über die Auferstehung Jesu Christi* (Einsiedeln, 1968), p. 70, where the writer stresses that we still do not know very much about the resurrection phenomenon.

though this is clearest in St. Paul's writings, is stamped by (a) a presentist mode of expression and (b) a futuristic one. To mention just a few characteristic occurrences of each: (a) God sent his Son as the old world order reached its completion (Gal. 4, 4); Christ brought us redemption while we were still sinners (Rom. 5, 8); now is the decisive moment, now is the day of salvation (2 Cor. 6, 2); (b) but the return of the Lord of this world, and his judgment, are not yet (1 Cor. 1, 7; 2 Cor. 1, 14; Phil. 3, 20f.; 1 Thess. 2, 19, etc.); mankind and all creation await, groaning in their hearts, the glorious freedom of God's sons (Rom. 8, 22ff.); Paul says he has not yet won the prize, not yet reached fulfillment (Phil. 3, 12ff.); Christ has yet to set the world free so as to bring it under his Father's rule (1 Cor. 15, 20-28).

This tight mixture of present and future is New Testament eschatology's most obvious characteristic.[4] Christ is the world's future in that he is himself approaching it in ever greater fullness. As it is in Christ that God approaches his creation, to that extent Christ is God's future (in Christ is all that is involved in God's future). Christ's death and resurrection herald the onset of God's rule over his creation. Through his Son, his final emissary, the creator initiates the process of giving true and eternal life to his creation. He is establishing his "new creation" (2 Cor. 5, 17). In Christ's resurrection from the dead God launched the new and ultimate creation, and to that extent his future is already present among us now (the present-orientated aspect of New Testament eschatology). But what has been begun still remains to be fulfilled in all things, is therefore in process and will one day embrace all creation (future-orientated aspect).

God himself is the future of man and of the world. Through Christ he approaches creation.[5] The Christ-event as a whole

[4] On this see W. G. Kümmel, "Die Bedeutung der Enderwartung für die Lehre des Paulus," in *Heilsgeschehen und Geschichte* (1965), pp. 36-47; R. H. Charles, *Eschatology* (New York, 1963); H. W. Kuhn, *Enderwartung und gegenwärtiges Heil* (1967); L. Mattern, *Des Verständnis des Gerichtes bei Paulus,* (1966).
[5] Cf. P. Stuhlmacher, "Erwägungen zum Problem der Gegenwart und

(death and resurrection) is a proleptic event: it has initiated and empowered a new and enduring order which it has situated within the temporal span. It is now growing to maturity and Christ is its driving force. What Christ has begun now develops in human history and reaches fulfillment in God, its future.[6]

II
THE MEANING OF RESURRECTION

The resurrection and glorification themes hold pride of place within the New Testament eschatological proclamation of faith. In the first place, both refer to Christ: God has raised him up from the dead and he is the Lord (Rom. 10, 9); God has raised him up among the people and has given him a name which is above every name (Phil. 2, 8ff.). In the order of that which is promised, however, both experiences are also applied to mankind: mortal and corporeal though we are, God will also raise us to new life through his Spirit who is in us (Rom. 8, 11); our bodies will be fashioned like his glorious body (Phil. 3, 21).

But what, in biblical terms, does resurrection mean? From what world of experience does the belief emerge? In what form did it originally arise and what was its ultimate development?

The cry "God is dead!" rings passionately through the cultic myths of the ancient East. Baal, the god of growth and fertility, sleeps the sleep of the dead during the summer dry season. Mot, the god of death, rules the people. With the onset of the rainy

Zukunft in der Paulinischen Eschatologie," in *Zeit. f. Theol, u. Kirche* 64 (1967), pp. 423-50; A. Grabner-Haider, "Welt und Mensch in Gottes Zukunft," in *Theologie der Gegenwart* 10 (1967), pp. 139-51; *idem, In Gottes Zukunft* (Einsiedeln, 1968).

[6] G. Sauter, *Zukunft und Verheisung* (Zurich, 1965); J. Moltmann, *Theology of Hope* (London & New York, 1966); *idem,* "Die Kategorie Novum in der christlichen Theologie," pp. 240-63 in *Ernst Bloch zu Ehren* (Frankfurt, 1965), pp. 240-63; W. Pannenberg, "Der Gott der Hoffnung," *ibid.,* pp. 205-25; K. Rahner, "Christentum als Religion der absoluten Zukunft," in *Christentum und Marxismus heute* (Vienna, 1966), pp. 202-13; E. Jüngel, *Gottes Sein ist im Werden* (Tübingen, 1965).

season, Baal rouses himself after a fierce struggle with Mot. A natural process is thereby made into a divine myth. But as the Old Testament shows us, Yahweh did not die. "Behold, he that keepeth Israel shall neither slumber nor sleep" (Ps. 121, 4), the psalmist sings, mocking the followers of Baal. Yahweh is a living God (Jer. 10, 10). The people of Israel are "sons of the living God".

In the earliest Old Testament books the underworld is the world of the dead, a land of no return that knows no human voice, only squeakings and murmurings, signs of a greatly diluted but continuing existence. The underworld implies permanent removal from Yahweh's face.

But gradually the belief arises that Yahweh is also Lord of the underworld. This is clearly the beginning of the biblical hope in resurrection. It takes on a more definite shape in post-exilic apocalyptic-eschatological literature and is in fact a response to Wisdom literature's despair in the face of death. "He [Yahweh] will swallow up death in victory; and the Lord will wipe away tears from off all faces; and the rebuke of his people shall be taken away from off all the earth" (Is. 25, 8). "Thy dead men shall live, together with my dead body shall they arise. Awake and sing, ye that dwell in the dust" (Is. 26, 19). Isaiah here is applying this hope only to the people of Israel: even their dead will be delivered from the shame of exile.

In Daniel 12, 2, this hope is expressed differently: "And many of them that sleep in the dust of the earth shall awake, some to everlasting life, and some to shame and everlasting contempt." This text represents a similar position to that held by the Hasidaeans.[7] Though it offers hope in resurrection even to the wicked, there is still no mention of resurrection for all. This extension, however, arises and becomes ever more strongly emphasized in the period immediately following the writings mentioned above. The history of religion shows that both in and

[7] See K. Schubert, "Die Entwicklung der Auferstehungslehre von der nachexilischen bis zur frührabbinischen Zeit," in Biblische Zeitschrift 6 (1962), p. 188.

outside the Bible, Jewish apocalypticism is the champion of hope in universal resurrection. Its basic testimony is: God is the Lord of the living *and* the dead.

And that is precisely what the New Testament proclamation says of Christ Jesus: Jesus is the Lord and God raised him from the dead (Rom. 10, 9). "For this reason Christ both died and rose again, that he might be the Lord of the living and the dead" (Rom. 14, 9). At first, Jesus' resurrection was proclaimed with almost unbridled enthusiasm until eventually there emerged from this exomologesis a formula that combined resurrection and death in the one proclamation: "Jesus is dead and is risen again" (1 Thess. 4, 14). The point is that it was the resurrection that so stimulated early Christian fervor, was seen as challenge and acclamation, and was then crystallized into a datum of belief.[8]

Another presentation of this theme, and the most immediate accounts of Jesus' resurrection, are contained in the gospels. They witness to the inexplicable nature of the resurrection event, though what they express is not as neatly done as in the formulas mentioned above.[9] In both, however, Christ's resurrection is seen as an event, even if only in its biblical meaning of *dabar*. Just as the world is created through God's word (*dabar*), or just

[8] Cf. H. Schlier, *op. cit.,* p. 9; V. H. Neufeld, *The Earliest Christian Confessions* (1963), pp. 120ff.; Ph. Seidensticker, *Die Auferstehung Jesu in der Botschaft der Evangelien* (1967), p. 11; *idem,* "Das antiochenische Glaubensbekenntnis in 1 Cor. 15.3-7 im Lichte seiner Traditionsgeschichte," in *Theologie und Glaube* 57 (1967), pp. 286-323; J. Kremer, *Das ältesta Zeugnis der Auferstehung Christi* (1966); G. Koch, *Die Auferstehung Jesu Christi* (1965).

[9] Cf. M. Albertz, "Zur Formgeschichte der Auferstehungsberichte," in *Zeitschrift fur NT Wissenschaft* 21 (1922), pp. 259-69; H. Grass, *Ostergeschehen und Ostergeschichte* ([2]1962); H. von Campenhausen, *Der Ablauf der Osterereignisse und das leere Grab* (Heidelberg, [2]1958); E. Fascher, "Die Osterberichte und das Problem der Hermeneutik," in *Der historische Jesus und der kerygmatischen Christus,* eds. H. Ristow and K. Mattiae ([2]1961), pp. 200-07; E. Lohse, "Die Auferstehung Jesu Christi im Zeugnis des Lukasevangeliums," in *Biblische Studien* 31 (1961); H. W. Bartsch, "Das Auferstehungszeugnis: Sein historisches und theologisches Problem," in *Theologische Forschung* 41 (1965); L. Goppelt, "Das Osterkerygma heute," in *Lutherische Monatshefte* 3 (1964), pp. 50-57; H. G. Geyer, "Die Auferstehung Jesu Christi," in *Christus under uns,* ed. F. Lorenz (Stuttgart, 1967), pp. 19-31.

as what God said to his prophets and his people actually came about, so also did Jesus' resurrection take place. It is God's deed, an event that is open to human experience and takes possession of its language. The event is the creative action of God's power and Spirit and it is formulated in terms of the two metaphorical expressions "awaken" and "cause to arise". The dead Jesus is assumed into the life-power (Spirit) of God.

The biblical witnesses go on to speak of "appearances" made by the risen Lord. "Appearances" (*ophthenai*) means on the one hand disclosure of a totally hidden mystery (*apokalypsis*), and on the other a human encounter and experience.[10] He who is risen encounters a person in the act of retiring from his view; he is experienced as one who is on his way elsewhere, as a wholly autonomous being. He discloses himself in language and in human life. The resurrection of Jesus occurred in the form of the risen Lord's testimony to himself, within human history and experience, just as *dabar* issues from God and happens in a human context. The crucified Jesus is encountered as the risen Lord. In this experience and encounter the crucified Lord discloses himself in the risen Lord and thereupon he withdraws once again; through the encounter we are permitted lasting awareness of his self-giving and his continuing existence for others.[11]

For the world as a whole, Jesus' resurrection signifies a turning point, the beginning of something totally new that possesses ultimate validity. A new era has begun in which man is enabled to reach his full human potential. "New life" (Rom. 6, 10f.), as reality and possibility, is now open to all men equally. In his resurrection, Jesus' death, which is for us all, turns into life for God and from God. Jesus' cross is now the way to life, a door that will never be closed. The resurrection discloses the cross' hitherto veiled life-force, existence for others and love. The world is put on a completely different basis and human life is

[10] H. Schlier, *op. cit.,* p. 38, uses the word "occurrence" in this connection.
[11] Cf. H. Schlier, *op. cit.,* p. 39.

transformed: Jesus' resurrection is the beginning of the general awakening from the dead, the onset of life's total victory. "Just as all mankind died in Adam, so in Christ all are given new life" (1 Cor. 15, 22). Christ is "the author of life" (Acts 3, 15), the "first-born from the dead" (Col. 1, 18). All creation is taken up into the new life of Jesus Christ (Rom. 8, 20ff.). Jesus died for all, representing us all; in his resurrection he conquers for all, representing us all. To each of us has been given equal opportunity for true life. Jesus' death for us is the conquest of death, and through his life, offered for us, he has become love itself. The culmination of God's kingdom is the acceptance by all men of this new life. God's future is attained through the universal attainment of the reality of the resurrection.

III

GLORIFICATION

In view of his resurrection, Christ is already and essentially "he who is raised up", which is to say he is already glorified. His resurrection was part of the process by which God took him to himself. This becomes clear in the hymn to Christ in Philippians where mention of Jesus' death leads immediately and exclusively to the mention of his exaltation: "He humbled himself and became obedient unto death, even death on a cross. Therefore God has highly exalted him and bestowed on him the name which is above every name" (Phil. 2, 8f.). The situation is similar in Luke: "Was it not necessary that the Christ should suffer these things and enter into his glory?" (Lk. 24, 26). From this we can conclude that originally resurrection and exaltation were independent interpretations of the same event. Jesus' entry into the life of the Father is seen in two different traditions: in the one case as resurrection and in the other as exaltation—that is, glorification.[12] In the passages just mentioned, Jesus' new life is in-

[12] *Ibid.*, p. 23.

terpreted in accordance with the structure of the Old Testament enthronement formula.

However, according to another tradition, resurrection and exaltation are regarded as correlative. Here the resurrection is the origin of exaltation; glorification and enthronement are the continuation and consequence of awakening. The epistle to the Romans would appear to confirm this: "It is Christ Jesus, who died, yes, who was raised from the dead, who is at the right hand of God, who indeed intercedes for us" (Rom. 8, 34); and elsewhere the same epistle says that Christ Jesus was "designated Son of God in power according to the Spirit of holiness by his resurrection from the dead" (Rom. 1, 2f.). Exaltation and glorification are therefore the object and consequence of the resurrection; the ultimate glorification of the Father occurs through the glorification of the risen Lord; this marks the fulfillment of his rule and dominion as creator of all (1 Cor. 15, 28). The theme of the glorification of God is central to and ultimate in Pauline theology.[13]

What, in greater detail, does "glorification" mean in its biblical usage? The Hebrew Old Testament uses the word *kabod,* meaning that which invests man with value and substance. In Sinai, Yahweh's *kabod* appears as fire (Ex. 24, 17); it shows itself to be terrible in punishment and indispensable in time of trouble (Lev. 9, 6. 23f.). *Kabod* is the "weight" (*gravitas*) of Yahweh, though it can also be interpreted as his power over the world which he wields as its Lord and creator. This dominion is expressed and exercised in human history (Ez. 3, 23; 8, 4; and elsewhere), but only at the end of time will it become visible as something bathed in glory (Ex. 43, 3ff.).[14]

In the Septuagint, Greek-speaking Jewry translated *kabod* by *doxa,* whose primary meaning is the glory and power of God, his splendor and beauty. Greek papyri and astrology give this word the additional meaning of dazzling brightness (brilliance) and

[13] On this see R. Bultmann, *Theologie des NT* ([5]1959), p. 353; P. Stuhlmacher, *op. cit.,* p. 449.
[14] Cf. R. Schackenburg, "Doxa," in *LThK* III, 2nd edition, col. 532f.

also use it to mean the magical power of the Godhead. For those who came directly under the influence of Hellenism, the word *doxa* could mean all these things.[15]

By the time the New Testament came to adopt the notion of God's *doxa*, it had been fundamentally influenced by Jewish apocalypticism. Here the divine *doxa* is seen as a specifically eschatological event: God will establish his dominion over all history (Eth. En. 25, 7); his will be a heavenly throne encircled by sparkling stars, cherubs and rivers of fire (Eth. En. 14, 8ff.); evil will melt before his face and the angelic powers will bend the knee in worship. But the just and the saints will also be clothed in God's *doxa* and their faces will reflect the brilliance of its light (4 Esr. 7, 97). Almost invariably, God's *doxa* is mentioned in connection with his dominion over all creation.

The New Testament shows that through his resurrection Christ received a share in God's glory. He is charged with the task of establishing God's dominion over all creation and for this reason is endowed with the power and the brilliance that belong to God in his glory. Through his resurrection he has become "the Lord of glory" (1 Cor. 2, 8); the Gospel as a whole proclaims the glory of God, emphasizes and highlights it (2 Cor. 4, 4). But Christ does nothing for his own glorification: the power he possesses is exercised solely to the glorification of the creator ("Jesus Christ is Lord to the glory of God the Father"—Phil. 2, 11). The Christ-event was the beginning of the glorification of God (Rom. 15, 7), and what Christ began must come to fruition in human history. Just as he was the first to share in the glory of the Father, so through him are all men to share in the same glory. Whoever, through Christ, obtains access to the Father may hope for a share in God's glory: "We rejoice in our hope of sharing the glory of God" (Rom. 5, 1-2). Whoever is willing to suffer with Christ and to further his life-purpose may hope to come into God's glory with Christ (Rom. 8, 18). Whoever,

[15] Cf. J. Schneider, *Doxa: Eine bedeutungsgeschichtliche Studie* (Gütersloh, 1932), p. 31; H. Kittel, *Die Herrlichkeit Gottes* (Giesen, 1934), p. 180; Von Gall, *Die Herrlichkeit Gottes* (Giesen, 1900), pp. 50f.

whether knowingly or unknowingly, has yielded to Christ and has confessed to faith in his life-giving cross, freedom and love, may hope for ultimate union with Christ in glory (Phil. 3, 20). By dying for mankind Christ became the first to enter into God's glory, and this possibility is now extended to all mankind. Christ is charged and empowered with the task of continuing in history what was begun through his death and resurrection—the establishing of the kingdom. Where Christ is, and where in us he comes to new life, the world is progressing into God's future.

IV

THE RESURRECTION AND
GLORIFICATION OF THE BODY

When the New Testament speaks of resurrection and glorification it is referring to the body. Christ's new life is a new life in the body and he lives on in those who confess his name ("the body of Christ"); he is glorified bodily (Phil. 3, 21). We, too, can look forward to the resurrection of the body in which our bodily form will be a permanent one determined by the life-giving power of God (1 Cor. 15, 44); man's physical body will be glorified and will share in Christ's bodily glory.

But what does the Bible mean by body, and in what actual context did it attain the meaning given it there? In Old Testament Semitic thought, man is an indivisible unity, and this unity is given him by the creator. Unlike hellenistic dualism, they did not see themselves as body and soul but simply as God-given life (*nepes*). The same unity characterizes New Testament anthropology. Here, especially in the Pauline writings, man is designated either as *sarx* or as *soma*. *Soma* is used in the context of resurrection and glorification, and it is an expression that in the Septuagint has no Hebraic equivalent to preserve the unity the New Testament writers intended to convey. Apocalyptic Jewish literature enriched the meaning of the expression by investing it with a significance peculiar to that genre. *Soma* was the whole man, formed by the creator, struggling between the forces of good and evil, a man of action and a social being and above all one who had to commit himself personally.[16]

Thus for St. Paul, man, in his "body" and in his "members", is the battleground on which is fought the struggle between sin, which leads to death, and righteousness, the new life to which God calls us (Rom. 6, 12f.). It is as physical beings that we embrace either the rule of Christ or the rule of sin (Rom. 6, 6; 7, 14; Gal. 6, 17). We encounter the world through our bodies, and the impact it makes on us occurs through our bodies. Existence in the world means existence in the body. As a physical creature of this world, a man's being is orientated toward that of others. Only through the body do we communicate with our fellow men. As a physical being, man always has two possibilities: he can either shut himself off from his fellow men, which will mean wedding himself to selfishness, or he can identify with them, which will mean realizing his dependent co-existence in the form of active love. The body is the whole man, who as such faces the necessity of deciding for or against God, of identifying with his brothers or rejecting them. The Bible does not regard man's physical existence as a passive condition but as one in which he experiences himself as man in an historical context and on the basis of his actions.[17] In the permanent facing of his decision for or against God he stands permanently open to the choice of new life, or death through sin. Christ's resurrection enables creation to reach its full potential. It was not just any death that led to resurrection, but only Jesus' death, for all mankind. Jesus' selfless existence led to new life. The resurrected Lord is new life to those who join themselves to him. He lives on bodily in those who choose to follow him in his freedom, obedi-

[16] Cf. E. Schweizer, "Soma," in *ThWB* VII, pp. 1064-91; J. A. T. Robinson, *The Body. A Study in Pauline Theology* (London, 1962); E. Käsemann, *Leib und Leib Christi* (Tübingen, 1933); *idem, Gottesdienst im Alltag der Welt* (Berlin, 1960), pp. 165-71; O. Cullmann, La délivrance anticipée du corps humain d'après le NT (Paris, 1946), pp. 32-40; P. Benoit, "Nous gémissons, attendant le délivrance de notre corps," in *Recherches de Science Religieuse* 39 (1951/52), pp. 267-80.

[17] Cf. E. Käsemann, *op. cit.*, p. 23.

ence and love. Men who await bodily resurrection await, in effect, participation in the infinity, glory, power and life of God (1 Cor. 15, 42f.). The New Testament goal is to see all men developing fully as such: they must not refuse new life but should embrace it. The hope expressed in the New Testament is that men will learn to live with and for one another, that God's love, revealed in Jesus, will come to fruition, and that the human race will be lifted up into the divine mystery.

V

PROLEPSIS AND ANTICIPATION OF THE FUTURE

With Christ's resurrection and glorification the anticipation of the future has begun. Not only are bodily glory and resurrection now possibilities open to all men but, more importantly, they are already in process. Resurrection as physical reality has been set in train, for the Spirit of God, who activates the process, is already active among us. He is given to those whose lives witness to God's love (cf. Rom. 5, 5; 8, 11). The Spirit, if one cares to look at it this way, is given to us as an advance payment against a binding contract. He who has received the Spirit may hope that what is begun in him will achieve fruition. The gift of the Spirit is the beginning of the redemption of the body (Rom. 8, 23). He who follows God in Christ is approaching resurrection. God's Spirit is the anticipation of the new life, of God's future for us, and he makes the bodily resurrection possible. Resurrection and the new, glorified body are primary features of a process of maturation that participates in the development of God's new creation. Where men through love open themselves to the Spirit, Christ incorporates them in his resurrected body.

In the same way, the glorification of the body is also anticipated, though the climax of God's glorification lies in the future (Rom. 5, 2; 8, 18). In Romans 8, 30, and nowhere else in his letters, Paul tells us that God has already glorified those whom he has justified. Here Paul is quoting from an early baptismal tradition which he has built into his own eschatology. Those who follow the creator's call are already endowed with his glory and so already reflect the glory of the Lord "with unveiled face" (2 Cor. 3, 18).[18] Through Christ's saving action the world is clothed in God's glory, with the result that "we all, with unveiled face, beholding the glory of the Lord, are being changed into his likeness from one degree of glory to another" (2 Cor. 3, 18).

Like resurrection, glorification is something already in process throughout the world. It began with Christ and will one day embrace all men. It does not continue of itself but only through us. We have to be open to the future so that we thereby become "fellow workers for God" (1 Cor. 3, 9; 15, 58). The future, as God's future, is a challenge to world and man: it is the challenge of the creator to his creation.[19]

Growth in God's new creation is impossible without our continuing collaboration. If man refuses to realize himself as a dependent social being, then bodily resurrection and glory are not anticipated. Thus we are urged to "glorify God in your body" (1 Cor. 6, 20). God's kingdom will be realized in this world and his glory will reside in our bodies and in our realized potential. For this reason the highest spiritual worship open to us is within the context of our bodily existence (Rom. 12, 1). There is, in fact, no other possible context. It is here, in this present form of existence, that the creator comes into his own and completes what he has begun. St. Paul sees our present mode of existence in terms of approaching resurrection and glory. Our bodily existence is orientated toward the new life of Christ, and so St. Paul perpetually urges us to cooperate in the work of the risen Lord (1 Cor. 15, 58). We are called to share in God's

[18] Cf. P. Benoit, art. cit., p. 276; B. Rigaux, S. Paul et ses lettres (Paris-Bruges, 1962), p. 190; St. Lyonnet, "La rédemption de l'Universe," in Lumière et Vie 9 (1960), p. 53; L. Cerfaux, Le chrétien dans la théologie de S. Paul (Paris, 1963), p. 249.

[19] Cf. my own account, Paraklese und Eschatologie bei Paulus: Welt und Mensch im Anspruch der Zukunft Gottes (Münster, 1968).

future, and in following this call it will be the extent of our commitment to our fellow men, to our own self-realization and to the renewal of the earth, that counts. On account of Christ's resurrection, human history has been given enduring value: bodily existence now implies potential and task, the anticipation of future resurrection and glory, openness to the future.

VI

SUMMARY

Central to the Gospel is the proclamation of Christ's resurrection and glory and the participation in these events that we may hope for. The proclamation of this theme has three basic component parts: message, challenge and promise. In the first place, resurrection and glory are beliefs proclaimed: Jesus is risen from the dead and has entered into the life of the Father so that he now rules with him. What has thereby been begun continues in human history, in that resurrection and glory are now open to all men. This message is also a challenge in that it demands a response from those who hear it. Because Christ is now at work in the world, suiting it to a new life, man is challenged to participate in this the Lord's work (1 Cor. 15, 58). This means that man has to be open to the new life God offers, submit himself to God's rule and witness to Christ's love.

Third, the message is a promise opening up for us undreamed of possibilities, the sole hope of true life and true self-realization. A new creation is developing which, though not made by man, cannot be made without him. All men are to be included in the resurrection of Christ and so all men are to come face to face with their creator.

Jesus' death on the cross, his death in obedient love, became the death of death, and so a new life. The world is therefore still evolving, and God has blessed it. Jesus' life and death for us became his resurrection. In the New Testament understanding,

Jesus' resurrection took place in human history through his appearance before witnesses,[20] in that through his encounters with them he finds new life in them. The same thing happens now, to the glory of the Father, wherever men express in their own lives the love and selflessness he showed, wherever his love is active in society.

Through Jesus Christ, resurrection and glory take place in human history because since the incarnation human history has been the sole context of God's self-revelation in Christ. But God is not absorbed by history: he confronts it;[21] we encounter the resurrected Lord precisely in the act of his withdrawal from us. The world is permanently challenged by the as yet incompletely realized achievement of the resurrection. This is not to say that Christ and world are alienated: on the contrary, he is situated firmly in our midst, for we and our world are destined to become God's new creation.

Thus Christ is God's future and therefore our future. Through Christ God approaches us and through Christ we discover ourselves. Christ is the attainable future.[22]

[20] H. Schlier, *op. cit.,* p. 39.

[21] J. B. Metz, "Gott vor uns," in *Ernst Bloch zu Ehren* (Frankfurt, 1965), pp. 226f.

[22] There is little that one can confidently say, on the basis of the biblical texts, about the intermediate stage in which each of us finds himself —between death and the general resurrection of the dead. Paul, in any event, expects to be united with Christ immediately after death (Phil. 1, 23). On this, cf. P. Hoffmann, *Die Toten in Christus. Eine Religionsgeschichtliche und exegetische Studie zur paulinischen Eschatologie* (Münster, 1966), pp. 341f.

José-María González-Ruiz/*Madrid, Spain*

Should We De-Mythologize the "Separated Soul"?

ecent studies in religious phe-
nomenology, history and sociology, and the questions raised by
Bultmann, have placed the problem of myth in the forefront of
theological debate. I am not going to plunge into the vast jungle
of the problem itself here, but I will try to use it as a starting
point for a correct approach to a theological and pastoral consideration of one of the aspects of our Christian "myth" which
would appear today to be in dire need of revision: the eschatology of the individual, which means the destiny of what until very
recently we called the "separated soul".

I

THE FUNCTION OF MYTH

It is undeniable that the history of human culture shows two
distinct strands. Man tries to understand himself and to seek the
stimuli necessary for the continuance of the human adventure. In
this quest for self-understanding there are clearly two directions
that at first appear contradictory. Each is defined by its own
model: the "scientific model" and the "mythic model". Bultmann
describes both approaches in a manner that could hardly be
bettered.[1]

[1] *Kerygma und Mythos* I, pp. 22-27; II, pp. 180-84.

The "scientific plan" starts from the supposition that the universe is complete in itself; it fits in easily with the συνεχές of Aristotle. The universe is not "pierced" in such a way that a supposed transcendence filters in through the chinks. It is true that cosmic "continuity" has recently ceased to be static and become dynamic, but it is still συνεχές.

The fact that working hypotheses change so rapidly nowadays is of no account; what always remains constant is the concept of the universe as a self-sufficient whole with no need ever to escape from itself or to project itself toward "something" completely outside itself, something "utterly other":

Modern scientific thought is not characterized by the content of its judgments on nature and the world, but precisely by the fact that no judgment on these matters can aspire to validity if it does not satisfy the demands of an adequate motivation. It is ignorance of the real difference between "mythological" thought and "modern" thought to oppose the contents of their different images of the world and to refer to the fact that "the modern view of the world" is considered partly as "discontinuous", "not closed" or subjected to complete transformation. This is not the point. The unbridgeable gulf between modern thought and mythic thought lies in the difference between unconsciously uncritical judgment and consciously critical judgment, even when the results obtained by modern natural science (reached, of course, on the basis of a consciously critical judgment) change in a few years. Representations of the images of the world succeed each other and they arise as hypotheses, but as hypotheses based on the critical responsibility of thought.[2]

This mythical approach has been shared by the men of every age. Mircea Eliade has described the reality of myth and at-

[2] C. Hartlich and W. Sachs, quoted by Bultmann in *ibid.* I, pp. 181f. Cf. A. Malet, *Mythos et Logos. La pensée de R. Bultmann* (Geneva, 1962), pp. 43f.

tributes it precisely to this intention of escaping from oneself, of transcending oneself, which characterizes civilizations with a religious stamp. Religious man assumes a humanity that has a transhuman, transcendent model. He sees himself as truly man only to the extent that he imitates the "external" and transcendent "powers". The religious man aspires to be *different* from what he finds himself to be on the plane of his ordinary experience. The religious man does not just *happen:* he makes himself, in the image of the divine models. He does see himself as *made* by history, but by sacred history, not profane history.

The non-religious, or profane, man, on the other hand, sees himself as made only by human history—that is, by a sum of "intranscendent" acts which give no impetus to create any higher model and which, consequently, lack meaning and stimulus for the religious man. In the "mythical approach" man is never truly man except when he conforms to the teaching of the myths, when he is imitating the gods.[3]

Now these two approaches—the scientific and the mythical—do not always run on parallel courses, but very often meet with a resulting osmosis between them. To take the mythical approach: one can see that man has a constant temptation to "rationalize" myth, thereby domesticating the supernatural "powers" and robbing them of the inevitable quality of surprise and discomfiture they possess in themselves.

G. van der Leeuw [4] has pointed out the way in which certain religious sects insist on giving a *name* to the god they worship. The name gives the divine power a definite outline and a specific content. When Moses asks God his name in order to justify himself to the rest of the nation, God replies with a "transcendentalist" evasion: "I am the God who IS. . . ." (Ex. 3, 14). The Romans distinguished the *dii certi* from the *incerti*. The latter were far more alarming. The only way of taming them was to build an altar to the "unknown god" (the *agnotos theos* of the

[3] Cf. Mircea Eliade, *The Sacred and the Profane* (New York, 1963), pp. 100f.
[4] *La religion dans son essence et ses manifestations* (1948), p. 142ff.

Greeks—cf. Acts 17, 22). It is this desire to rationalize myth that Bultmann calls "mythology"; so to "de-mythologize" is to "de-rationalize", to denude the essence of the myth of the *logos* of rational man who tries to neutralize and assimilate any "otherness" that he feels threatens him—that is, any *real* otherness.[5]

From this it follows that the true function of myth is to "let pass", to serve as a channel for direct communication between the conscience of the believer (or the community) and the supernatural power, which always presents itself as "completely different", "utterly other".

Jürgen Moltmann has found a felicitous description for the "atheism" (?) of Ernst Bloch as an "atheism for God":[6] the "atheist-for-himself" does not think of God as the utterly other or the utterly changing one, since he considers himself to be god; the "atheist-for-God", on the other hand, destroys all the religious images, traditions and feelings in himself that formed an illusory link between himself and God, precisely because of the inexpressible vitality of the God-who-is-utterly-other.

Thus, mythology is precisely the attempt to destroy the "otherness" of God, to make him cease to be "other" and become something approachable, something that belongs to us. It is an attempt to domesticate God, to free oneself from the insecurity occasioned by his gratuitous, and so disconcerting, presence. *When this happens, myth ceases to be transparent and becomes opaque.*

The real task of de-mythologizing is not aimed at the destruction of myth, but at restoring its transparency. This involves looking less at the myth in itself and more through its restored transparency. This would be the positive achievement of "trans-mythization" or the return to myth as a way, though inadequate, of expressing the ineffable.

It is in this sense that I want to examine the old Christian myth of the immediate eschatology of the individual—the "separated soul". It can hardly be doubted that there has been a real

[5] Cf. A. Malet, *op. cit.* p. 57.
[6] Ernst Bloch, *Religion im Erbe* (1967), pp. 8f.

"mythologization" of the myth—valid in itself—of the individual's encounter with God beyond the limits of personal life. I shall therefore try, following the biblical thread, to discover the content of the myth in order to give it back its transparency and at the same time its authentically religious validity.

II

THE GREEK VIEW OF THE MYTH OF SALVATION

An outline of Greek thought on the subject of immediate personal eschatology is useful for an understanding of the religious content of the myth, since it formed a background and provided a contrast to the rethinking of the myth carried out by the authors of the New Testament. Popular expressions of Greek thought can be left on one side, but the philosophy of the great thinkers had a profound influence on the writers of the New Testament and on early Christianity.

In Platonic metaphysics, as is well known, the soul is not only immortal, but eternal. It is a spark of the divine fire, which knew the world of sovereign ideas "before", and which later—for reasons that are not always very clear in the Platonic tradition—was cast down from the heights and encased in a human form, where it is a prisoner and an exile, though without losing its imperishable nature.

Plato distinguishes three parts in the soul: the seat of the lower passions, the seat of the generous passions and the seat of the intelligence. Only the last of these is immortal. Aristotle apparently diverges from Plato in considering the soul as a form of the body, without which it would be unable to carry out its vital functions.[7] But it is not easy to fit Aristotle into a "materialist" mould. In fact he talks of a "soul of another kind", the intelligence, the Νοῦς, the principle of thought, which is certainly

---

[7] "As the soul is the ἐντελέχια of the body, it cannot exist without a body; it is certainly not a body, but is something of the body": *De Anima* II, 2, 413, a. 12.

based on the body, but without intermingling with it. It is a sort of "superform" which directs the activities of the "form" of the body. This Νοῦς is immortal and represents what is divine in man.

We should not imagine that the thought of these two giants blossomed in an existential desert; on the contrary, the ancient and widespread Orphic tradition offered fertile ground on which to cultivate this view of the soul as divine and immortal. The Orphics considered the transcosmic journey of the soul as an unfortunate trip through the "wheel of sorrows". The soul that finally escapes from this circle returns to the world of the gods. It has its own passport to this world in its divine origin, its intimate belonging to the gods themselves.

On a gold tablet, found in a tomb on Patelia, the dead Orphic says: "I am a double being, half heavenly and half earthly" [8]— or even more simply: "Earth to earth, spirit to heaven." [9]

This dualism logically led to a devaluation of the body, which came to be considered as the tomb of the soul—σῶμα σῆμα.[10] The dualist tradition was continued by the Stoics. The early Stoics admitted that the soul lived on, but seem to consider it an impersonal immortality. It is immortality of a "cyclic" nature, since one day the world will be reabsorbed within the Principle that animates it, in a "universal conflagration" which will be succeeded by a "regeneration" that will reproduce the cosmos in a form identical to its previous one. But among the Roman Stoics the doctrine of immortality evolved in a more "personalist" direction and took on a religious tone very similar to that of Christianity. But dualism still lived on: man was made up of two totally opposed elements—the body, which belongs to the earth, and the spirit, the sovereign moral principle, which comes from God and goes back to him.

---

[8] εἰπεῖν: γῆς παῖς εἰμι καὶ Οὐρανοῦ ἀστεροέντος, αὐτὰρ ἐμοὶ γένος οὐράνιον: A. Dieterich, *Eine Mithrasliturgie* ([2]1910), p. 8.

[9] Γᾶ μεν ἐς γᾶν, πνεῦμ'ἄνω: E. Rhode, *Psyche* II (Mexico, 1948), pp. 389, 257ff.

[10] Plato, *Gorgias,* 47, 493A.

<h2 style="text-align:center">III</h2>

<h3 style="text-align:center">THE MYTH OF INDIVIDUAL SALVATION IN THE BIBLE</h3>

For a correct understanding of the biblical myth of individual eschatology, one has to start from the presupposition that for all the authors of the Bible—the Old as well as the New Testament—there is no such thing as the "soul" in the sense in which it is found in Greek thought. The biblical man is one unit. But what is even more important to emphasize is that, according to the Bible, there is no divine element in man which guarantees the survival of human personality after death.

The word that is used, *nepheš,* which is incorrectly translated by "soul", means the vitality of man in its broadest sense, and it is expressly stated to be subject to death (Num. 23, 10; Jud. 16, 30). In the biblical concept, what matters is to present man—the whole of man—as a reality completely distinct from God. Man in himself is "flesh". "To be flesh" in the Old Testament implies a double dimension.

One—the vertical one—refers to God. *Bāsār* opposes the creature to the creator, stressing his weakness and mortality, limitations compared to the attributes of God. "Flesh" is visible, God is invisible; "flesh" is limited, God is infinite; "flesh" is powerless, God is all-powerful; "flesh" suffers, perishes and dies, God is immortal.[11]

The second dimension of the flesh-man in the Old Testament is horizontal: "flesh" not only designates each man in his isolated individuality, but humanity as such, man himself, seen as belonging to a more or less homogenous collectivity. In the texts just referred to, this communal aspect of "flesh" is emphasized. The expression "all flesh" (*kōl bāsār*), which appears over and over again, clearly refers to humanity as such, to the historical condition of a group of human beings, however extensive.[12]

[11] Gen. 6, 3; Ps. 78, 38-39; Is. 40, 6; Deut. 5, 26; 66, 16; Jer. 12, 12; Ez. 21, 9-10.
[12] Cf. Gen. 6, 12; Eccl. 14, 18; 33, 21; Is. 40, 5-6; 49, 26; etc.

St. Paul builds up the whole of his theology of man on the basis of this Old Testament conception. "Flesh" for him designates the human-earthly being as such, seen in his weakness and mortality, in contrast to God and his "Spirit" (Gal. 1, 16; 1 Cor. 15, 50; Rom. 9, 7-8). This meaning—originating in the Old Testament, as H. Mehl-Koehnlein has shown [13]—is further extended and even surpassed by the use of "flesh" to imply the whole sphere of human existence, everything in the created world that touches man or concerns him in any way, everything that bears his mark or the stamp of his dominion, everything that is humanized through contact with man. Man's existence and mode of being are not circumscribed and enclosed by corporeality, by the individuality proper to each person, but are shown and realized in a much broader sphere, in which man participates and over which he exercises responsibility. In a word, man in the Bible is (1) a unit, and (2) fragile, corruptible and mortal.

The overcoming of this feeble mortality can only be achieved through the "breath" or "Spirit" of God, which is always presented as a free gift. The "Spirit" in the Old Testament is always a gift of God and the only possible means by which beings can be incorporated in the sphere of "life".[14] As G. van Leeuw writes:

This is the Christian concept of the destiny of man, in spite of many contradictory concepts within Christianity itself: "The free gift of God is life eternal in Christ Jesus our Lord" (Rom. 6, 23), and "This is eternal life, that they know thee the only true God, and Jesus Christ whom thou hast sent" (Jn. 17, 3). It means that the soul is not some immortal goddess, but merely a position in relation to God. It means that neither understanding nor moral act has any influence on the destiny of man, but only God himself. It means that eternal life is given to man, but not that it belongs to man: it belongs to God. Certainty about the

[13] *L'homme selon l'apôtre Paul* (Neufchatel-Paris, 1955), p. 14.
[14] Cf. E. Jacob, *Théologie de l'Ancien Testament* (Neufchatel-Paris, 1955), pp. 131ff.

beyond can only be derived from experience of the divine love: *nihil longe est a Deo, neque timendum est, ne ille non agnoscat in fine saeculi unde me resuscitet,* as St. Monica said (*Confess.* IX, 11). The destiny of man, whatever it may be, is based on the love of God. This explains the magnificent concept to which Dante gave expression, that love also created hell (*Inf.* II, 4ff).[15]

Thus, on the basis of this understanding of man as "flesh", as essentially mortal and liable to corruption in the whole of his being, the inrush of the "Spirit" of God was seen as a free gift, but at the same time as a reality present in the run of human existence. Man was *in fact* marked by this invasion by the divine Spirit. This is why death was considered as something negative and antagonistic to the action of God. A dead body represented the final grade of impurity for the men of the Bible (Num. 9, 6; 16, 18; 31, 19)—hence the ritual measures taken to protect oneself against all contact with mortality and corruption.

G. von Rad writes: "The result of all these measures is a radical de-mythologization and de-sacralization of death. The dead man was placed right outside the context of worship of Yahweh, and Israel was not to know any other form of worship. The dead were separated from Yahweh and from all living communion with him, because they were outside the walls from within which worship was offered to Yahweh (Ps. 88, 11-13). The bitterness of death lay in this fact, and the Psalms of lament express it in a most impressive way." [16]

This outlook clearly shows that, for the biblical mentality, being close to God always means being close to life and far from death. This is the ultimate basis of the Judaeo-Christian myth of individual eschatology.

[15] *Fenomenología de la religión* (Mexico-Buenos Aires, 1964), p. 325.
[16] *Théologie de l'Ancien Testament* (Geneva, ²1967), p. 243.

IV
GOD IS ONLY A GOD OF THE LIVING

We are now in a position to understand the argument of the
"living God" that Jesus uses so naturally in support of the resurrection of the dead: "And as for the resurrection of the dead,
have you not read what was said to you by God, 'I am the God of
Abraham, and the God of Isaac, and the God of Jacob'? He is
not God of the dead, but of the living" (Mt. 22, 31-32).

Throughout the whole Bible, God appears as the "giver of the
Spirit"—that is, he who promises life to beings who in themselves
are corruptible and whose natural end is death.

It is true that God appears as creator and as Savior in the
Bible, but there is a sort of *dialectic antagonism* between these
two dimensions. God is creator precisely because he creates a
world completely different from himself, completely *other*. In the
profoundly beautiful phrase of Athenagoras, "between God and
the world there is a great abyss".[17] Creation, rather than bringing the world nearer to God, distances it from him. In particular,
man is left to exercise his free will and charged with carrying on
the work of creation. The deep significance of God resting on the
seventh day can only be seen in this context (Gen. 2, 2-3). This
affirmation in the Bible tends to exorcise the world, stripping it of
the spirits that people it in other religious schemes.

And then this God the creator, this God who has placed such
an abysmal distance between himself and the world, gratuitously
offers to be present in it, but this time *as a Savior*. God comes to
save: this is the great affirmation the Bible makes about the
divine presence in human and cosmic history.

Man recognizes his own insufficiency and is not content with
it. This experience is the initiation into the presence of God,

[17] "Ἡμῖν δὲ, διαροῦσιν ἀπὸ τῆς ὕλης τὸν θεόν, καὶ δεικνύουσιν ἕτερον μέν
τι εἶναι τὴν ὕλην ἄλλο δὲ τὸν θεὸν καὶ τὸ διὰ μέσου πολύ. . . , μή τι οὐκ
ἀλότως τὸ τῆς ἀθεότητος ἐπικαλοῦσιν ὄνομα: *Suppl. Pro Christianis* 4.

what the Councils of Orange were to call the *initium fidei*. God then presents himself offering salvation. And salvation is always referred to the overcoming of mortality. Salvation is always concerned with life.

The whole history of the faith of Israel is an upward journey toward a better understanding of "life" as a gift from God. A. T. Nikolainen rightly states that Yahweh's power over death is the presupposition for the resurrection of the dead.[18] R. Martin-Achard [19] sums up his study in this way: "We have seen that in the Old Testament faith in the return of the dead to life is based in the last analysis on Yahweh's revelation to his people. It was due to the fact that the God of Israel manifested himself as a powerful, just and good God that the *hasidim* affirmed the return of the dead to life. The event that Christians celebrate at Easter equally sanctions, in their eyes, the greatness, justice and mercy of the God of Israel and of the Church: the resurrection of Jesus is a witness to the triumph of the living God over the forces of evil (Acts 3, 15; 4, 10; 10, 40 etc.), a witness to the divine justice that offers salvation to sinners and transforms them in the image of the Son of God (Rom. 4, 22ff.), and reveals to those who believe the love of the Father from which no one can separate them, and the care of Christ who intercedes continually for them (Rom. 8, 34ff.). Easter is also the confirmation of Yahweh's revelation to his people; the faith of the apostles is united to the hope of the *hasidim;* just like Israel, the Church depends on God's promises for her hope in the death of death, but with this difference: the Church knows that death has already been overcome, and so praises Jesus Christ, against whom hell no longer has any power, because he has, once and for all, opened the way of eternal life to men."

Therefore, faith in the resurrection is precisely the same as faith in the saving God. For the biblical writers, there is nothing divine or immortal in man: he is all mortal. God alone, through

[18] *Der Auferstehungsglaube in der Bibel und ihre Umwelt* (Helsinki, 1944), pp. 113f.
[19] *De la muerte a la resurrección* (Madrid, 1967), p. 236.

his saving power, can offer man the opportunity to overcome his innate mortality.

Furthermore, God is conceived of only as saving. This, in the minds of believers, is the only reason for his existence. What this means is simply that God is not a God of the dead. The God who as a matter of *fact* made himself known to the minds of believers is a God who offers life over and above innate human mortality. He is the God of the living. The reason why, long after the time of Abraham, Isaac and Jacob, he is still presented as their God, is that these patriarchs, who were great believers, have in some way overcome, or are in the process of overcoming, human mortality.

Seen in this light, I would consider Barth's proposition, which many theologians initially found very disturbing, valid: "For Paul, the expression 'resurrection of the dead' is nothing more than a periphrasis of the word 'God'." [20] Of course the equation is valid as long as one does not attempt to "rationalize" it, as it would appear that Barth himself does in his attempt to "situate" the *eschaton* outside time and space. According to the great Swiss theologian, the eschatological resurrection of man does not come through a progressive evolution or a catastrophe; it comes through "the life and death of men; it is the history of salvation following its particular course through the other history".[21] Equally, the *parousia* "has not taken place in *any* time, because it is the mystery, the basis and the eternity of *all* times".[22] The two—resurrection and parousia—are one and the same and take place "in the eternal instant, in the *now* in which past and future cease: the past ceases going, and the future, coming".[23]

I would say that according to the strict logic of faith, we believers cannot allow ourselves the luxury, as Barth does, of placing the form and manner in which the saving God is going to

[20] *Die Auferstehung der Toten*, p. 112.
[21] *Ibid.*
[22] *Römerbrief*, p. 402.
[23] Cf. J. M. González-Ruiz, *Epístola de S. Pablo a los Gálatas* (Madrid, 1964), pp. 305ff.

fulfill his promise of enabling us to overcome mortality either inside or outside space and time.

V

CONCLUSION

This is the only valid stance the believer can take before the "myth" of individual eschatology. What happens between the moment of individual death and the full realization of the divine promise with regard to the overcoming of death? Does a part of man stay in a sort of state of hibernation waiting for all the others to arrive so as to make up the full establishment of the definitive People of God, the people of the redeemed?

There is no denying that in our Christian tradition and in the successive ecclesial formulations of our faith we have built up a whole structure of theological imagery to give us some sort of answers to our anguished questions. Are these answers valid? Should we be undertaking the task of "de-mythologizing" our formulations, even the dogmatic ones? I think this is essential. If we are agreed on the importance of serious work on the de-mythologization of the Bible, why should we resist the inevitable de-mythologization of dogma?

Biblical de-mythologization does not tend to destroy myth or even to replace it; it only tends to restore its transparency, so that it can again become *only* a clear means of transmitting the re-vealed message.

Naturally, de-mythologization of dogmatic formulae would not have to strip away the eternal truth behind each formula, but only its ecclesial truth, or rather its ecclesial-historical truth. The Church, under the impulse of the Holy Spirit, has been telling herself her own faith throughout her history, formulating it in the language of the time and trying to understand the revealed mes-sage as it appeared to her at any particular time. "But the Word of God is not fettered" (2 Tim. 2, 9), not even by the space and time of ecclesial modes of being. The Word of God is always present, new and fresh from the oven, as it were, at each period of the Church's history.

Today the Church is rethinking her faith in the saving God and is finding, or will find, new formulas in which to express this faith. This does not mean that she *has to* renounce the old historical formulas, but they must in no way be built up into the "Word of God". The Word of God does not congeal, but goes on flowing through the whole history of salvation.

Believers today have reached a higher degree of maturity and see no need to exercise their imaginations on details of "how" God acts from the culminating moment of each person's death. They believe in a God who saves and are prepared to give him a "blank check" to act in the form and manner in which he thinks best.

And yet, of course, we belong to the Church, and those of us who are convinced Catholics are not going to cut our links with the ecclesiastical magisterium. On the contrary, we have such confidence in her that if she should at any given moment offer us a new dogmatic formulation, we are not going to be annoyed or waver in our faith. We have given the Church a blank check too. We know that what matters is to believe in the living God of Abraham, Isaac and Jacob, and to believe that this God is not a God of the dead, but of the living.

"Where there is hope, there is religion," Ernst Bloch has said.[24] Our hope in a saving God, waiting for us beyond the finite limit of our mortality, is what makes religion exist in the world. This is what unites believers in one Church. We know that within the prophetic ambit of this Church this hope will continue to be defined and expressed. At the same time we must beware of two "rationalist" dangers: the first is to elevate theological imagery (the ecclesial myth) into a sort of quasi-scientific reply to the rational questions of man; the second is to try to replace the anachronistic myth by another more "rational" one that may satisfy—but not for long—the aspirations of modern man.

To sum up: a continual work of de-mythologization makes us

[24] *Das Prinzip Hoffnung* (Frankfurt, 1959), p. 1404.

attentive to the authentic content of our faith—hope in a saving God who will welcome us at the frontier of our existence in the manner he deems fit, if we have fulfilled our mission to be "servants of the living God".

Meanwhile, we live in trust in the lap of our Church and follow her advice and recommendations, without requiring this to mean that she has exhausted all the possibilities of her understanding of the Word of God.

Piet Schoonenberg, S.J./*Nijmegen, Netherlands*

I Believe
in Eternal Life

"Through Christ you have confidence in God, who raised him from the dead and gave him glory, so that your faith and hope are in God" (1 Pet. 1, 21). That our faith is at the same time hope is very clear when we confess: "I believe in eternal life." That is why this article of faith is particularly relevant in our present "theology of hope". On the other hand, Western man is today more skeptical than ever about a "hereafter". This article deals first with eternal life insofar as it means "future", both within history and beyond it, not merely for the sake of tactics but for reasons of principle. Only after this will it treat of eternal life as God's promise of a life hereafter. I shall try to show this expectation of eternal life as possible and as evidenced by Scripture. Finally we shall see whether in this life we can already trace some lines the projection of which will allow us to speak meaningfully about the content of eternal life.

God Gives Us a Future

Biblical hope tends toward a future, but a future which has already started and is rooted in the present. The Reformed theologian H. Berkhof stresses this important aspect in his book *Gegronde Verwachting.*[1] When Nathan tells David that Yahweh

[1] H. Berkhof, *Gegronde verwachting. Schets van een christelijke toekomstleer* (Nijkerk, 1967).

97

will build him a house, this building has already been started by God's giving him the throne over his people. But this promise is above all founded on what God has done and still does for his people in the past as in the present. The recognition of this forms the context of Nathan's prophecy in 2 Samuel 7. The prophets frequently recall the deliverance from Egypt as a guarantee of the future. It almost disappears in Proto-Isaiah to make room for the "burning present", but in Deutero-Isaiah the first exodus becomes the image of a second one which is about to take place. As Karl Rahner has explained so effectively, prophecy is not a reporting back from the future but an unfolding of the promise which lies embedded in the past and the present of God and man.[2] The apocalyptic approach obscures this factor but does not contradict it when we look at it more closely. Its detailed descriptions of the judgment and the new aeon are too improbable and particularly too incoherent to be understood as literal information about the future, information which would reach us by way of God's omniscience and eternal present. The fact that the apocalyptic literature sprang up practically everywhere in a situation of oppression does not prevent it from being ultimately rooted in God's covenant through which the oppressed people were aware of being "the people of the saints of the Most High" (Dan. 7, 27). This relation between past, present and future is no different in the New Testament. The kingdom of God as preached by Jesus is no doubt a thing of the future, but it is also "near" (Mt. 4, 17) and "among you" (Lk. 17, 21). In John the eternal life which today we identify so easily with the hereafter is already present now, just as the judgment is already taking place now (see, e.g., Jn. 3, 18. 36; 5, 24; 6, 47).

If the future of God rests on a present within our history, then it cannot be a future detached from history. For if God's salvation is really operative within history, it is bound to have some meaning for this history and must have a future within this his-

---

[2] K. Rahner, "Theologische Prinzipien der Hermeneutik eschatologischer Aussagen," in *Schriften zur Theologie* IV (Einsiedeln, 1960), pp. 401-28.

tory. This is confirmed by Scripture. In the Old Testament this future was for a long time exclusively conceived as taking place within this world: the dead who have gone to *sheol* are no longer part of it. In the New Testament the gifts of God bestowed on us in the Spirit through Jesus constantly urge action and are part of the building of the future. If this future is little considered at the human level in the Bible, it is because of the limited view of what man can do that was prevalent in those days. And so the New Testament gives us no plan for economic improvement or the abolition of slavery. But now that we feel that we hold the future in our own hands, we should again go back to and reflect upon the present meaning of God's promise for this world in the Old and the New Testaments. This promise of God is today particularly relevant precisely insofar as it embraces indiscriminately both the hereafter and our present history.

The relevance of this insight inplies two things. First, this present and this historical future must be the immediate object of the Church's preaching, and she must direct her service particularly to this present time. Without this, the last word of the Christian message, the promise of a life beyond death, will become incredible. And this is not merely because contemporary man happens to be so vitally interested in this world but also because of the very nature of the situation, since we cannot genuinely put our trust in God for the hereafter unless we can rely upon him here and now and for the immediate future. This is the more so because, for all the fulfillment that is involved, we and our world will be the same in the ultimate future as in the history of this world. Second, it means that we can only discuss these things with those that deny a hereafter or find that it is not worth bothering about when both sides have seriously thought about God's future within the framework of our present history. Even with the far from negligible differences about the hereafter there is room for a Christian and even universally human ecumenical dialogue about hope.

Within such an ecumenism we begin by thinking about what it

means that it is God who gives us hope (and this implies thinking about what we mean, and what appeals to us, when we talk about "God"). This is also the basis of the dialogue with Marxists, where the notion of an "absolute future" plays an important part.[3] Let us look at this future in the light of the whole relationship between God's activity and that of man in this world. God is never our rival, nor a substitute, but always has the initiative; indeed, he is the initiative. Far from leaving us out of it all, God wants us to be beings who plan and build their own future. Although in the Old Testament God's salvation is often attributed to his intervention (only the stories of Joseph and Esther show his guidance within a causality of this world), the prophets are far from being limited to a mere foretelling of a fate or destiny. They not only call for a response that will be rewarded by God, but also for definite actions by which man molds his own future, as, for instance, when Jeremiah urged an agreement with Babylon (Jer. 27 and 29). The love of neighbor, too, whether in Deuteronomy or in the New Testament, is directed toward the building of a better future. Without excluding the beings that are his creatures, God has the initiative because all that is created derives from him. His particular initiative lies in the grace which constantly urges us to be true partners in his covenant, in the Spirit who makes us his children in Christ, and thus each other's brothers and sisters. This initiative is full of surprises. "My ways are not your ways" (Is. 55, 8): this saying does not refer to the mystery of the acceptance of evil in God's plan but to the generosity with which he constantly forgives it and the power with which he mends the consequences. He can always go further than our deeds and even our thoughts: "He can do infinitely more than we can ask or imagine" (Eph. 3, 20). In the light of this expectation the Church can always prophetically criticize whatever man does or plans to do, on condition, of course, that she herself remains subject to the criticism of God's Word. She

[3] See, e.g., the symposium organized by the Paulus-Gesellschaft, *Christentum und Marxismus-heute* (Vienna, 1966), with the essays by K. Rahner, "Christentum als Religion der absoluten Zukunft," pp. 203-13 and J. B. Metz, "Zukunft gegen Jenseits?" pp. 218-28.

can point out shortcomings and urge more humanity in all our ideals for the future. But, more than criticize, she must preach the promise. God has always prepared more than we can imagine, and so we may never give up hope, whether because of disillusionment or because of an inclination to rest on our laurels. God's future cannot be fenced in by human boundaries.

Beyond Death

God also gives a future beyond death. The possibility can hardly be denied if we accept God as truly God; the factual promises are in the scriptures. But here modern Western man boggles, and his doubts, his silence, his attempts to shut it out or deny it, are bound to affect the believer. First, we should try to understand why the message of an eternal life beyond death simply fails to come across today. One may say that the technical-minded man of today is above all an empiricist, and this need not be a "value-judgment". If his empiricism becomes exclusive, we have here one of the reasons why our scientific and technological concern with this life ousts the interest in the transcendental —i.e., in the transcendency of God and his gifts.

But there is also a philosophical reason why we think that death is the end of everything. Death is taken far more seriously in our present anthropology; one might say that it is seen as something ontological. Plato's view of man as composed of a mortal body and a soul which, insofar as it transcends this body spiritually, is immortal, a view partly corrected by St. Thomas with the help of Aristotle, is subject to criticism, and by the same token the hereafter loses its credibility. The soul no longer passes through the death of the body. Not only the new Dutch catechism but before it Karl Rahner had pointed out that soul and body die together.[4] One may even add, with Leo Bakker, that the soul or the spirit of the person is what dies most in man.[5] This ontological seriousness of death makes it appear as a radical

[4] *A New Catechism* (London/New York, 1967), pp. 470-76; K. Rahner, *Zur Theologie des Todes* (Freiburg, 1958), pp. 37f.
[5] L. Bakker, "Geloven in verrijzenis," in *Bijdragen* 28 (1967), p. 316.

end to all. Our age seems to ignore the psychological aspect of
death but to take the ontological aspect very seriously (the latter
perhaps explains the former).

But all these theories do not even mention the principal argument against a hope of a hereafter: the protest against an exchange of this life for eternity, the alienation of our task on this
earth. On this point practically everyone agrees today with
Feuerbach and Marx and we must take their criticism very
seriously.

Christians who are led by these arguments to a hushing up or
denial of the hereafter can appeal to both the Old and the New
Testaments. The Torah only knows of a blessing or punishment
by God within the framework of this world, and this is why the
Sadducees, who only accept the Torah, still denied the resurrection in the days of Jesus and St. Paul (Mk. 12, 18; Acts 23, 8).
The prophets indicate God's promise in their prediction of a
restoration of the people which will be like a resurrection from
the dead (Ez. 37, 1-14), but it is a collective resurrection. That
everyone will have a part in this begins only to appear in the
apocalyptic literature (Dan. 12, 2f.) and has become a conviction in 2 Macc. 7, 9. 14. 23. 29. 36). The wisdom of Proverbs is
still wholly conceived in terms of this life, just as in the Deuteronomy collection "life" and "death" are both forms of existence
on this earth while the act of death itself is usually taken as nor-
mal. For the author of Ecclesiasticus death is a threat but the joys
of this life are God's blessings. It is true that Israel does not usually
see individual death as a vanishing into total nothingness, but the
sheol is nevertheless constituted by a lack of all that fills life:
strength, enjoyment of the fruits of one's labor, communion with
fellow human beings and even with God. Like the chaos before
creation this sheol after this life can be called a "void" for all
practical purposes. Only very rarely does God's power seem to
penetrate into that region or does his faithfulness toward us
reach beyond death. In the Wisdom literature only the book of
Wisdom itself, chronologically the last of that collection, clearly
shows the same conviction as Daniel and 2 Maccabees, and it

does this in a curious mixture of the Greek idea that the soul continues to exist and the Jewish apocalyptic notion that immortality is a gift contained in the resurrection (Wis. 3, 1-4).

Leaving aside the Greek formulation, this conviction became common in Palestinian Judaism where it became particularly one of the tenets of Pharisaism. It is therefore easy to understand why Paul, remaining a Pharisee on this point (Acts 23, 6), lays so much stress on Christ's resurrection as well as on ours in 1 Corinthians 15. As Willi Marxsen suggests in *Die Auferstehung Jesu als historisches und als theologisches Problem*,[6] one can see in this view of Paul the Pharisaic way of interpreting the active continuity of Jesus' message and call ("Die Sache Jesu geht weiter"—the affair of Jesus goes on).

Marxsen also mentions another way of interpreting this— namely that one is sent in order to continue what Jesus has begun, naturally in close connection with the person of Jesus. One might add here that the oldest eucharistic theology, as found in the same Paul (1 Cor. 11, 24-26), does indeed speak of "remembering the death of the Lord", but it makes no mention of the presence of his person. For these and other similar reasons one may wonder whether, within the context of belief in Jesus Christ, there is no room for both a Sadducean and a Pharisaic interpretation of Jesus' influence. Is not the only new element of the New Testament the person of Jesus Christ, so that all the attitudes for which there was room in the Old Testament belief in God could also exist legitimately in the belief in Christ? If this can be accepted, a purely "this-worldly" Christianity is also legitimate, and this has already been accepted as a matter of fact for a long time within Protestant liberalism and is gaining ground also among Catholics. In such a Christianity the hope of eternal life would not alienate us from building a future on this earth, while the memory of Jesus' example, constantly revived in Christian preaching, would remain an inspiration for us to do just that.

[6] W. Marxsen, *Die Auferstehung Jesu als historisches und als theologisches Problem* (Gütersloh, ⁵1967).

But within the framework of that "universal ecumenical approach" I mentioned above, I would, nevertheless, like to defend the personal resurrection of Jesus and the promise of a personal, eternal life beyond death as an essential element of the Christian faith. For this there is no need to cling to a dualism within man (such a dualism is in any case simply the acceptance of a certain complexity within man). If the whole man, and even his spiritual personality, dies, this does not necessarily exclude *a priori* that the whole man can exist in a life after death in a state of fulfillment. It is true that such a life cannot be described in terms of our present condition, whether we speak of the risen Christ or of ourselves. It has even become more difficult to imagine than in the past so that we have to proceed with the greater caution when we try to argue the continuity of a personal existence on philosophical grounds. Perhaps we can only prove the ineradicable desire for this continuity and so point to the ontological possibility. In that case our belief in God's promise of this eternal life will have to be the bolder for that reason. The objection based on alienation has already been dealt with, at least in theory, because we started with the hope of a salvation which, without futher qualification, starts from within history and then transcends it. This theoretical reply to this mainly Marxist objection must of course be constantly put into practice, and this is one of the most serious obligations of the Church today. We can only preach our hope of a God-given hereafter in a credible manner if we build up this present life in our trust in him.

From the mere possibility I turn to the scriptural, especially New Testament, promise of an eternal life beyond death, realized first of all in the risen Christ. The variegations of attitudes and insights on this point in the Old Testament cannot absolve us from taking this fact of salvation in the New Testament and the promise linked with it very seriously. In any case, is this pluriformity in the Old Testament so imposing in itself? First of all, the fantastic presentation of the "other" life in the apocalyptic literature or the Hellenistically-influenced description of it in Wisdom in no way necessarily diminishes the authenticity of the belief in and hope of eternal life in itself. This belief and this hope are rooted directly in the belief in a saving God. We may say that this belief is the only element which makes Israel and Judaism differ in religious matters from their cultural environment, but we must add at once that this faith gradually changes and renews everything that is taken over: worship, the view of nature and history, and ultimately also the view of death and the hereafter. God's salvation is so vast that we can also personally build on it. The God of Abraham, Isaac and Jacob, of the burning bush, is not a God of the dead but a God of the living. The passage where this argument (*ad hominem,* because it is taken straight from the Torah itself!) is used against the Sadducees (Mk. 12, 18-27) may or may not use the exact words of Jesus during his life on earth, but it is certain that it contains the exact Christian and Jewish value judgment about the development which has taken place in the Old Testament. The Catholic Church may therefore be glad that in her acceptance of the Old Testament she has not relied exclusively on the Palestinian canon.

Moreover, the question about the Old Testament canon need not cause any divisions in the Church because belief in the eternal life is unequivocally expressed in the writings of the New Testament—in the passage just referred to, and in all that is said about Christ's resurrection and his return. Insofar as 1 Corinthians 15 is concerned, Marxsen is right in saying that Paul sees the resurrection of Jesus as a special instance of the general resurrection (see esp. vv. 13 and 16). But he overlooks what is special in the case of Jesus. For it is here not a case of a resurrection on the last day but a resurrection that has already taken place in anticipation so that Christ is the "first-fruits" also in time (1 Cor. 15, 20-24). Moreover, one can point out that there is a possibility of personal contact which does not coincide with meeting a historical person. When Marxsen understands by resurrection a fact within human history which can be established and verified by historical methods, he may rightly say that such an interpretation cannot be binding. One may even go further and say that it is a wrong interpretation. The disciples were not anxious to "establish" something but rather to arrive at a personal faith. And this happened precisely through the way in which Jesus made himself recognizable, communicated with them and made himself personally present to them. Even Marxsen senses this personal presence of the risen Lord when he says that the "affair of Jesus" does not go on as if his person is no longer involved, and certainly not as if we can carry on without him.[7] It is precisely the person of the risen and glorified Jesus who in his Spirit (for "the Lord is the Spirit": 2 Cor. 3, 17) constantly summons us and gives us the strength to spread his message and to continue his work of deliverance.

It is therefore true that the Jewish expectation of the resurrection interprets the events of the life of Jesus, but the inverse is still more true. Christ is indeed "risen according to the scriptures" (1 Cor. 15, 4), but conversely it is the encounter with him as risen which interprets the scriptures, as is very prominent in Luke (24, 27. 45). Of the New Testament, too, one can say that the person of Christ is the only new element, but here, too, one must add that he changes all things and makes all things new. This applies also to the remembrance of him. Where this remembrance of Jesus is celebrated, his death is announced but without excluding his resurrection. In any case, what is peculiar to the eucharistic proclamation of the death of the Lord is that it takes place "until he comes" (1 Cor. 11, 26). That he will come means that he is alive, even though this was provisionally understood as "being kept in heaven" (Acts 3, 21). Just as in the Old Testament God was too great to be a God of the dead, so the presence of God's salvation in Jesus made him the Living One forever and ever (Apoc. 1, 18). It is precisely in this that he is "the first-fruits of all who have fallen asleep" (1 Cor. 15, 20).

How Should We See the Final Fulfillment?

In speaking about eternal life, I do so fully conscious of the fact that we have no information about it. We can only start

[7] Marxsen, *op. cit.*, pp. 26 and 34.

from eternal life as we have received it *now* in the glorified Christ, and on that basis we can try to see beyond death. The concepts we use are both positive and negative, just as our concepts about God. We apply the perfections of our world to God, but stripped of all creaturely limitations, so that we speak stammeringly about God with words that begin with "all-" and "in-" such as "all-wise" and "infinite". Therefore, when we speak about eternal life, we must again start with our earthly life; eternal life is therefore a fullness of what is earthly but without earthly limitations such as mortality, suffering, de-personification, the crumbling into bits and pieces of time (see, e.g., 1 Cor. 15, 42-44). And so the life about which I am going to speak cannot be called crudely the here*after,* since this expression puts this life and the other life in the same kind of temporal sequence. Moreover, this whole language, like that which we use for God, is not exclusively and primarily a speaking-about but rather a speaking-to. To speak about God is to acknowledge him, and to speak about the final fulfillment is the confession of our hope, even if there are no words for it. Even Scripture stammers here and needs many images to indicate God's final gift. We shall briefly look at these scriptural images and here and there link them with questions that people ask today.

The risen Christ is he who is glorified. He is filled with that quality which the Old Testament attributes to God: glory, *doxa, kabod,* splendor, the luster that radiates on all. Thus our earthly existence will also pass into a glorified existence, an existence of fulfillment through participation in the "glorious" and "resplendent" life of God. What else can we say about it? It is a communion with God who "is all in all" (1 Cor. 15, 28). All this plainly points in the direction of a community. On earth we see mankind grow into a world community, and so the final fulfillment is a projection of this. However, it remains impossible for us to picture it to ourselves, not only because of the total absence of enmity, but also because this community will fulfill man in depth in a way undreamt of in our philosophy. If, according to the Gospel (Mk. 12, 25) marriage is excluded from heaven, it certainly does not exclude personal love and the bodily expression of it. The image of the feast is filled out with that of the sabbath rest which, like God's own sabbath rest, is not non-activity but the fulfillment and celebration of creative activity. The relation to God finds particular expression in the texts which say that we shall know as we are known and that we shall see God face to face (1 Cor. 13, 12). This certainly means an un-thought-of encounter with God.

The Greek preference for *theoria* or contemplation has put a heavy stress on this vision in the post-biblical tradition. It may indeed help us to understand the greatness of our final fulfillment but we ought to beware of one-sided approaches. First of all, this vision of God is certainly not seeing God as an object or a fathoming of his being. It should rather be sensed as a seeing of his face, based on the fact that he shows himself to us and sees us. It is therefore an interpersonal communion with God which must be expressed just as strongly in terms of love. And so, this vision and this communion in love cannot exclude the creation and certainly not our fellow human being. To put this immediate vision of God *alongside of* our communion with creatures and creation is a questionable procedure. When in a medieval definition Benedict XII speaks about an intuitive vision without the intermediate instrumentality of any creature whatever and stresses the immediacy of this vision of God (DS 1000), this rightly excludes any earthly mediacy. We no longer know God through his creation, through reasoning. It is rather the intuitive element of all knowledge and certainly of all belief which is brought to its full flowering, and thus we stand before God, not outside but in the midst of his creation. Today it is already our ideal to meet God *in* his creation, and our problem is whether we really meet *him* there. We may say that it is precisely this problem which will be solved in a way we cannot imagine. In *God's Creation*, A. Hulsbosch has linked this vision again with the world and the brother, which seems to me a great step forward.[8]

[8] A. Hulsbosch, *God's Creation* (London, 1965), pp. 197-226.

What I have said so far about the final fulfillment shows that I see it as a personal fulfillment. The blessed are persons, "personalized" to the fullest degree. This means first of all that they are not merely the substance of remembrance in those that remain behind. Continuity in memory is a specific human value but it dies within history. There is a continuity at a deeper level which consists in the continuity of a person's influence, particularly when this was a good influence. The promise of eternal life beyond death implies that this influence is not merely carried on by others and is therefore exercised by others, but that it continues to go out from the person himself. The image of the community shows that we must understand the fulfillment of the person also as conscious and free, although, at the same time, as unimaginably linked with the personality of others. We might say that we are truly and totally open to others only when we have reached this fulfillment. The inalienability of every individual is not destroyed, but personality consists precisely in the highest degree of self-communication. In this we are related to the others and to this earth, however difficult it may be to represent this to ourselves. One might call this the glorification of our corporeity. When Paul speaks in 1 Corinthians 15 about the glorified body, he refers to the whole person: it is nowhere distinguished from a soul. In a moment I shall come back to the meaning of this distinction between soul and body in the hereafter.

This blessed fulfillment can be gambled away. We are told this explicitly in Jesus' threatening words about the judgment, particularly in Matthew.[9] Paul seems to open up a perspective of a final fulfillment for all.[10] This idea can be found in tradition, particularly that of the Eastern Church, and especially in Origen's teaching of apocatastasis. Augustine, however, speaks of a number, even a large number, of damned, and his influence determined Western thought. Probably these two currents of

[9] Cf., for example, Mt. 7, 23; 23, 33; 24, 51; 25, 12. 30. 41. 46.
[10] Rom. 5, 12-21; 11, 30-32; 1 Cor. 15, 22. 28; Eph. 1, 10; 1 Tim. 2, 4; 4, 10; cf. 1 John 2, 2.

thought should not be mutually exclusive. We are faced here with the mystery of the unfathomable reality of both God and man. Hell is a possibility in us, and redemption is a still greater possibility in God.[11]

When we talk about the final fulfillment as *eternal* life, we must beware of an abstract and impersonal notion of eternity. The biblical notion of eternity does not give us much more than an immeasurably protracted time, something of which we cannot see the end. Philosophically we can exclude from the notion of eternity both beginning and end as well as every form of succession, at least every kind of succession which implies imperfection. But this definition, inspired by Boethius, does not describe eternity in itself but God's eternity. Man, however, is a creature of time, and when we talk about human eternity we mean a fulfillment of the temporal condition which is inherent in his being. As Berkhof says of the glorified Christ, our eternity lies in the fact that "past, present and future form a new synthesis".[12] This means that a certain growth also remains possible in this final fulfillment. Otherwise we would perhaps cease to be human. Just as life constantly gathers itself from the past into the future, so we shall constantly rediscover our past and our present in and from God in new and surprising ways.[13]

[11] Cf. K. Rahner, "Theologische Prinzipien. . . ," *op. cit.*, pp. 420f. Precisely because damnation is preached only as a possibility (however seriously), the scriptural description of it is very incoherent. Side by side with the apocalyptic analysis of God's punishment (e.g., Apoc. 14, 10f.) we have the vision of Wisdom 5 according to which the punishment of sinners consists in the recognition that they have lived in vain. Moreover, in Scripture the resurrection is sometimes universal, sometimes reserved to the just (compare e.g., Jn. 5, 29 with 1 Cor. 15). This latter view allows for the opinion that man is not immortal by virtue of his humanity. This in turn allows one to see hominization not only phenomenally but also ontologically as a slow process of micro-mutations, where it is difficult to draw a sharp line between man and animal.

[12] Berkhof, *op. cit.*, p. 31.

[13] Hulsbosch, *loc. cit.*; L. Boros, "Entwurf einer philosophischen Eschatologie," in *Orientierung* 25 (1961), pp. 252-54; 26 (1962), pp. 4-7, 30-32.

This last point implies something that is relevant for the possibility of an "intermediate period" between death and parousia. This period will be a time during which we grow into the final fulfillment of all. Thus the elect are involved in the adventure of our history, rejoice in the coming of God's kingdom and suffer through sin. They suffer particularly through those sins which have not been wholly overcome in their own being or perhaps those sins of theirs which have contributed to "the sin of the world" and have not yet been extinguished in the world. This last point especially can help us to understand the Church's teaching that the souls still need our prayers and love in their purification. Sometimes Protestants think mistakenly that for Catholics purgatory coincides with the whole intermediate period.[14] On the other hand, Catholics may think of purgatory as an intensification of the progress of the dead toward total salvation. A moment ago I mentioned "souls", and the Apocalypse speaks in Chapter 6 about "the souls underneath the altar". These are not, however, waiting for their bodies but for the fullness of the number of their brethren. And when Paul speaks in 1 Corinthians 15 about the rising of the bodies, this is not contrasted with separated souls, as has already been said. It seems to me, therefore, an open question whether the separate state of the souls in the intermediate period is a matter of Christian teaching or of anthropology.[15] I prefer the latter and think that "corporeity" grows, not in the biological sense but in the anthropological sense of growing through the growing communion with all. In his *Zur Theologie des Todes,* Karl Rahner has spoken about the "soul becoming wholly cosmic" at death, and this would be followed at the parousia by a new corporeity.[16] It seems simpler to

[14] Berkhof, *op. cit.,* p. 76.

[15] It does of course belong to the language used in dogmatic definitions; see esp. DS 1000: "etiam ante resumptionem suorum corporum" (even before they reassume their bodies).

[16] K. Rahner, *Zur Theologie des Todes, op. cit.,* pp. 17-26. Rahner sees this cosmic character of the soul as an inner disposition toward the glorified body, and this glorified body as the expression of the soul's openness to the whole cosmos.

me to say that this cosmic expansion is already the developing of a new kind of corporeity in the *biblical* sense, so that we are already growing toward the resurrection during the intermediate period.[17]

[17] Hence the expression used on p. 472 in *A New Catechism:* "They are about to rise".

Samuel Rayan, S.J./*Ernakulam, India*

The Eschatological Hope of Hinduism

I

HOPE FOR LIFE EVERLASTING

Deliverance from death seems to have been the overwhelming preoccupation of ancient Hinduism. The following verse expresses the yearning and defines the hope of those days:

> Lead me from the unreal to the real;
> Lead me from darkness to light;
> Lead me from death to immortality.[1]

The text proceeds to explain that the unreal and darkness are death, the real and light signify immortality. The sage Yajnavalkya is questioned by Maitreyi, his wife: if the whole earth belonged to me, should I be immortal by it? What should I do with that by which I do not become immortal? And by Aśvala: since even sacrifice is subject to death and decay, by what means is the sacrificer freed beyond death? And by another: death eats up everything; what god will consume death itself? [2] The special boon young Naciketas would demand of Yama, god of death, is

[1] *Brhad-aranyaka Upanisad* 1.3.28. These references may be looked up in Robert E. Hume, *The Thirteen Principal Upanisads* (Oxford, 1921); S. Radhakrishnan, *The Principal Upanisads* (London, 1953).
[2] *Brhad. Up.* 2.4.2-3; 3.1.3; 3.2.10-13.

knowledge of the mystery of death and of the hereafter.[3] And so the quest goes on; immortality is ever the pressing concern. Brahman, the Absolute, is regularly described as the immortal, and those who know him become immortal.[4] In the *purāna* (mythology) period this quest was enshrined in the central story of the churning of *amrta-sāgar,* the ocean that held the nectar of immortality.

II

AN HISTORICAL SURVEY

Vedic times enjoyed the assurance of endless personal immortality in the paradise of the gods, and the *Brāhmanas* nurse the same hope except that one of them hints at rebirth for those who perform rites incorrectly.[5]

In the age of the *Upanisads* the object of hope was described as union with the Absolute, resulting in perfect immortality, supreme freedom and ecstatic bliss. Sometimes a personal immortality is meant, sometimes impersonal absorption into the divine Transcendent.[6] This state of bliss is commonly called *Mukti* or *Moksa* (release, liberation—deliverance from *Samsāra,* the cycle of rebirth). Upanisadic thinkers forged the old idea of retribution into the inflexible law of Karma (action), according to which every deed leaves its traces on the doer, and bears a harvest of joy or sorrow for the doer to reap. Karma dispositions or residual propensities of previous births are carried by causal

[3] *Katha Up.* 1.1 and 1.2.

[4] *Katha Up.* 1.3.15; 2.3.1; 2.1.1; 2.3.9,14-17; *Brhad. Up.* 2.5.1-14; 3.7.3-23; 3.5.1; 4.4.7-21; *Chandogya Up.* 7.23 and 24; Jabal Up. 3; *Mundaka Up.* 2.2.12; 3.2.5,6,9; *Kena Up.* 2.4-5; Śvetaśvatara *Up.* 3.1,7,13; 14.20,17.

[5] *Rgveda,* I.25.6; X.1.3.; 6.10; ix.41.2; *S. Das Gupta, A History of Indian Philosophy* I (Cambridge, ⁴1957), pp. 25-26; S. Radhakrishnan, *Indian Philosophy* I (London, 1940), pp. 113-16. Śatapatha Brahmana, 1.6.3.1,4.

[6] *Chand. Up.* 2.20.2; *Prasna Up.* 6.5; *Munda Up.* 2.2.2; 3.2; *Katha Up.* 2.15; S. Radhakrishnan, *The Pricip. Up.,* p. 119; idem, *Indian Philosophy* I (1940), pp. 236-39.

bodies which determine the circumstances of every birth. On
coming into contact with causal bodies, souls which are eternal
pure spirits set out on their *samsāra* voyage; they acquire in
addition subtle bodies which are the subject of experiences, and
gross bodies such as we see.[7] When the gross body falls off, one
dies. But as long as the other two bodies remain attached to it,
the soul must repeatedly come to birth till, through this discipline
of *samsāra* and the knowledge of Brahman, all *Karma* is con-
sumed and overcome. It may take thousands and thousands of
births and deaths before the liberating discernment should dawn
upon the soul.[8]

The systems deriving from the *Upanisads* preserve the eschatological perspective given above, but each uses the vagueness of
ancient texts to introduce its own color and emphasis. One interpretation is pure *advaita* or non-duality, openly monistic and
solipsistic. In it there can be no room for eschatology or hope.
There is only an apparent process of recovery of self-identity by
the only reality that exists, through the fading off of a non-
existent illusion of duality and otherness. Śankara's position
might appear to be somewhat similar. Much indeed in his writings is suggestive of monism.[9] Mukti is realization of the Atman
(Self) and of the Brahman (the Absolute); now Atman and
Brahman are identical and one in essence; the sense of otherness
comes of ignorance, and the world is a dream, an illusion. The
hope therefore of liberation centers on an illumination that will
chase the shadows and bare the truth of one's identity with the
Absolute. All this is true, but it is also true that Śankara's
thought is complex, with his concept of world-God relationship
finely shaded and nuanced. On this relationship rests the meaning of End-time and of the hope that bears on it. For Śankara the
world is no mental fiction, is neither being nor non-being, but
being-nonbeing; it is a dynamism coming from God and seeking
him abroad, and approaching its own ideal self in the measure in

[7] *Chand. Up.* 5.10.7; *Śvetas. Up.* 5.11-12; *Kaushitaki Up.* 1.2.
[8] *Brhad. Up.* 6.2.15; *Munda. Up.* 3.15; 5.7; *Svet. Up.* 1.7; *Kaush. Up.*
1.2.
[9] S. Radhakrishnan, *Indian Phil.* II, pp. 580-81.

which it approaches him. Each moment and event therefore of this evolving universe is an approximation to the Eschaton, and a fresh breath of hope—that is, existentially. Formally, however, Śankara prescribes knowledge as the means to *Moksa,* and his presentation shows it is hard to come by except for the elite.

For Rāmānuja and his school, *Moksa* is a state of perfect bliss experienced in Brahma realization and the full blossoming of one's own existence; for, "man's true nature consists in belonging to God as his body".[10] The Self remains in God but as a distinct personality which adores and loves the supreme Person. Release is effected by his grace who has power to plan and realize his purpose, who, as Lord of *Karma,* can cause its accessories so to be collocated as to fructify in a way that will give his mercy a chance to lead us out of bondage. Thus all can be saved and the world process can come to an end. At the moment of liberation the soul will shed all matter connected with it, for such association is a degradation for pure spirits. That, however, does not mean matter is evil; it has meaning as the medium of life in which to expend the karma force and as the body of God, and a sort of pure matter serves liberated souls as the medium of communication. Do we have here an adumbration of the communion of saints and of the consummation of the world? [11]

The hope that Madhva seeks to sustain is similar to Rāmānuja's. Liberation comes through direct realization of God and is the work of his grace. Before release as well as after, man remains distinct from God: he is not God nor of God, but *for* God. His true nature is to be a servant of God, delighting in his worship. Difference in bliss and privilege among liberated souls is a cardinal point in Madhva's teaching. There are four aspects of release: *sāmīpya,* closeness and intimacy with the Divine; *sārūpya,* similarity of nature with the Divine; *sālōkya,* co-existence with the Divine in the heaven; and *sāyujya,* communion with the Divine through entrance into and self-identification with his

[10] P. Sankaranarayanan, "The Nature and Destiny of Man from the Hindu Point of View," in *Religion and Society* VII (1960), p. 66.
[11] S. Das Gupta, *op. cit.,* 3, pp. 292-95; S. Radhakrishnan, *Indian Phil.* II, pp. 683-86, 703-15.

body of bliss. Madhva limits both man's hope and God's grace in adding that gods and superior men deserve liberation; the lowest sort of men and demons always suffer in hell, while ordinary men continue on the way of rebirth.[12]

The *Bhagavadgīta* is willing to collect and hold all the traditions current in its day about the goal and hope of life, but it also has a preferred conception of its own. *Moksa* consists in coming to Krsna and abiding in him. Those who seek him with devotion will surely find him, and those who come to him will have their bonds sundered, and they will live in him in peace and joy, for he is the ultimate rest of the universe.[13] This hope reposes not so much on human merit and endeavor as on Krsna's love and promise:

Think on me, be devoted to me, worship me and bow to me; so shall you surely reach me: this I truly promise you, for you are dear to me.[14]

Krsna's love concerns itself not only with the salvation of men but with the welfare of the world. The world, too, may then share his grace; the world, too, may then come to Krsna. Though supremely free and perfect, Krsnna keeps working for the universe, and would have us work, too, for such selfless service does not forge fetters for the spirit. The possibility is here open for involvement even of liberated souls in the world's affairs, and so for the world to enter more and more into conditions of *Moksa*.[15]

Since Krsna descends into the world, the End becomes present to world processes;[16] he comes not to cancel it, nor to take the good out of it and leave it then to its dark doom; he comes to give it more being by liberating it from forces of evil and promoting forces of righteousness and growth. The Hindu doctrine of

[12] S. Radhakrishnan, *op. cit.*, pp. 743-748; S. Das Gupta, *op. cit.*, pp. 4, 315-19.
[13] Cf. *Bhagavadgita*, 4.9,10; 6.15,30,31,47; 7.23; 8.7,16,21,28; 9.4; 11.18,38; 18.54,55.
[14] *Bhagavadgita*, 18.65,66; cf. 18.58,68; 8.5,7; 9.34; 12.8.
[15] *Ibid.*, 3.20-24; 5.25.
[16] *Ibid.*, 4.7-8; 12.4,13,15.

Avatāra (descent) for all its imperfections holds within it a germ of hope and creates within history an eschatological situation. Krsna breaks into history whenever dharma (duty, religion) begins to decline, and he comes to act, to protect, to destroy. In the view of the Gītā, history is not an even flow and time is no mere chronological succession. History has its high points, its moments of opportunity and crisis, its crucial hours of encounter and decision. Not every hour is like every other: there are God's hours and favored peaks where the divine appears, active to save. Neither are all the moments of grace alike, for Kuruksetra and the hour of the Gītā revelation are unique. The Gītā sustains the sense of the endlessness of history by presenting Krsna as Kāla, Time. He is endless, changeless Time, the devourer of all time. Our days and years and the world's ages slip through our fingers but are gathered in him and kept secure for us. He is the End into which all flow, and he is the beginning and the middle from which all come and in which all are held together.[17] In Gītā and in much Hindu thought time is structured as all eschatological time is that carries within it a maturing hope. In popular belief there are times propitious and otherwise; the hour of death is particularly important: a right attitude then can undo a whole aggregate of evil *Karma* and secure release. The institution of the four Āśramas (student, householder, hermit, mendicant) is a conscious attempt at meaningful structuring of time for the maturation of life. Somewhere at the basis of such conceptions lies the experience of time as eschatological and moving toward a consummation.

Taking now these presentations as a whole, we note that from the Vedic period to the Upanisads there has been a deepening of thinking on the shape of life into which our present existence is to issue. From the Upanisads through the Gītā to Rāmānuja there has been a significant development of thought. The vital points Rāmānuja has made are the clear affirmation of the permanence of the individual personal self in the state of release, and the primacy of bhakti and love in the constitution of *Moksa* and of

---

[17] *Ibid.*, 10.33; 11.21-23, 25-31; 10.20.

the path that leads to it. Both points ring authentic and modern. We are today becoming increasingly aware of the centrality and significance of the human person, as well as of love and the relations—human and divine—that love builds. The thought of Rāmānuja and the Gītā is also capable of further completion and development. These two names are picked out for mention, for theirs seem to be the deepest intuitions in Hinduism in the matter of eschatological hope; they are the points of growth for tomorrow. One question in which rethinking is unavoidable would be the place assigned to the body in the constitution of man, and consequently the place to be given to human activity and achievement in the final consummation. If man is saved in his totality, then the whole thinking body that he is must participate in the grace of *Moksa* as well as the entire thought-body that is his, namely his history, his culture. These too will have to be led into the presence of the Lord. And that brings us to the question of the universe. That the world is meant ultimately, together with men, to become the body of God is a fascinating insight which calls for elaboration and further probing. No less attractive and worth pursuing is Rāmānuja's suggestion of communion among the released mediated by "pure matter". Finally we feel that the entire problem should be thought out afresh in vital link-up with the whole ferment of modern life.

III
MODERN TIMES

Hope in India today is bound up with programs of development and nation-building. From the national will to grow a new sense is coming to birth of the value and moment of the material world. The world is no longer felt as alien to man but as his body, as part of his very life and self, as that in which he lives and realizes himself as an individual person and as society. A new sense of community and corporate action and common destiny is also taking shape among us. National development is impossible without collective effort, and mankind's problems call for world collaboration. Mankind is one, and is saved or lost as a unity. This sense of togetherness is brought home to us daily by the impact of international politics and trade as well of modern media of communication which are fast reducing the world to a close neighborhood. There is in the third place a new awareness of history, its unity, movement and meaning, and together with it a new appreciation of time.[18] Time is not uniform but progresses through crises which compel decisions and movements which are irreversible. History and time are no longer conceived as cyclic but as progressive, spiralling onward, heading for something momentous. And on that account the weight of each point of time is beginning to be felt. As the hours and minutes are charged with moment and decision, a sense of urgency is taking hold of the country, an impatience to press forward, to produce results, to achieve things and to grow up plan by plan. There is therefore a new commitment to earthly tasks, to science and technology, to humble service of the brother.

These new spiritual attitudes are rich in hope and large in eschatological dimensions. Planning for development and the process of nation-building imply a philosophy, a goal-oriented, eschatological view of life. The new outlook is fast taking hold of the soul of India, and Hinduism is accepting it, not of course without pain and an experience of death. In the process it is getting transformed without losing its identity. Modern Hindu thinkers are busy reinterpreting and reformulating ancient beliefs and positions without in any way feeling that they are the less Hindu for it or the less loyal to tradition.

A relevant example would be the central problem of the destiny of the cosmos and its inclusion together with man's historical eschatological hope. In none of the classical explanations has the world a chance of salvation; at best, its destiny is left

---

[18] See such titles as K. M. Panikkar, *The Determining Periods of Indian History* (Bombay, 1962); P. Sankaranarayanan, *Values of History* (Bombay, 1962).

uncertain. Today, however, Hindu thinkers neatly place the
world within the purposes of God and discern in its accelerating
historical process the pressure of the Eschaton. S. Radhakrsnan,
for instance, insists that in the state of *Moksa* the world of
plurality is not dissolved or abolished, but continues to exist and
function. It is we that change in our attitude to the world. With
the advent of a new insight our false outlook drops, all alienation
is overcome, and we give to the world a new value. We come to
see that the world is neither Reality nor illusion, but the appearance of Reality, its image, its translation on the plane of space
and time. We realize that the world is a becoming, a movement
and struggle toward Being, Reality, God. Samsāra is a process of
transformation into *Moksa*. It is always becoming what it is not,
always transforming itself by ever closer approximations to the
Infinite. It exists therefore in eschatological tension. Its consummation will come when absolute liberation will be achieved
for all. When the purpose of the cosmos is thus fulfilled, "the
cosmic process is taken over into that which is beyond all
manifestations".[19]

The seeds of this development may be found in Rāmānuja's
acceptance of the world as the body of God, and his assigning of
"pure matter" as the medium of communion among the liberated. Basis may be found also in the Gīta view of history as
constituted not merely by an even, flat, flow of time, but by
moments of divine intervention, opportunity and crisis.

Roots of these new developments may be traced back even to
upanisadic visions. According to Iśa Upanisad, to cross death
and attain eternal life you need both avidyā and vidyā, this world
and the next. You need to live in this life according to its conditions and its tasks, and keep an eye on him who envelops all.
Those who attend only to prayer and God to the neglect of the
world, enter into darkness; into greater darkness enter those
who attend to the world and forget God. We must understand

---

[19] S. Radhakrishnan, *Ind. Phil.* II, pp. 563-64, 566-86, 637; *idem,
The Pricip. Up.* pp. 127-31; *idem, The Bhagavadgita,* p. 78.

and we must worship; we must be loyal to both the manifest and the unmanifest, to this world and to God, to work and to contemplation.[20]

The hope of Hinduism has today expanded to include in its range the material world and human history with all man's endeavors and achievements. The implications of this new position have not yet become articulate in the heart of Hinduism. However, someday it will, and on that day there will be surprise and joy in that heart and in other hearts as well.

[20] *Iśa Up.* 1, 9-14.

PART II
BIBLIOGRAPHICAL SURVEY

Gerhard Sauter/*Gottingen/Mainz, West Germany*

The Future: A Question for the Christian-Marxist Dialogue

R eflection on the future provides a far-reaching link between contemporary Catholic and Evangelical theology. Accordingly, there is a common reappraisal of the Marxist concept of the future. On the other hand the most noteworthy feature of modern Marxism would seem to be its outlook on the future. In relation to this, its traditional view of history and its political economic theories fall into the background.

The State of the Dialogue

Recent years have seen the beginnings of dialogue between Christians and Marxists. The stage has now been reached when this dialogue is an obvious part in the contemporary intellectual scene. The conditions for this dialogue are often created in part by historical presuppositions. Conditions are most favorable where there have been prior associations between Christians and revolutionary groups, as where the Hussite heritage helped to prepare mutual understanding. In other countries, especially in Latin America, changes are appearing in the political attitude of the Church. Vatican Council II, with its attitude to atheism in Schema 13,[1] may not have created readiness for dialogue, but

---

[1] Cf. G. A. Wetter, "Kirche und Kommunismus," in *Die Autorität der Freiheit* (Munich, 1967), pp. 590-95; H. Gollwitzer, "Das Gespräch des

certainly greatly encouraged it. This readiness found an important echo in the three disputations between theologians and
Marxist theoreticians organized by the Society of St. Paul in
Salzburg in 1965, in Herrenchiemsee in 1966 and in Marienbad
in 1967. Wider publicity will now be given to the exchange of
views between Marxists and Christians through the international
journal, *Convergence,* first published in 1968 by an ecumenical
editorial group. The Protestant World Study Conference on
Church and Society which met in 1966 in Geneva coined the
slogan "the theology of revolution", having especially in mind
developments in Latin America and Asia.[2]

The contacts already established [3] have facilitated the exchange of information and frank discussion of problems, which
either touch on common interests or were formerly the occasion
of persistent misunderstandings. Special mention must be made
of the efforts to achieve genuine understanding between the
partners through detailed exposition of their total outlook. Thus
the Prague philosopher, Milan Machovec, has prepared a study,
"Marxism and Dialectical Theology",[4] and the "Philosophy of
Hope" by the German Marxist, Ernst Bloch, has been widely
taken up in theological circles,[5] or been analyzed and answered
by theologians.[6] Marxist modes of thought and problems have
been introduced by Roger Garaudy and Henri Lefèbre to French-
reforming Catholicism, and by Herbert Marcuse to the American
theologian, Richard Shaull of Princeton. In all of this the problem of the future is central.

Konzils mit dem Atheismus des Ostens," *ibid.,* pp. 596-603; H. Flügel,
"Der atheistische Marxismus als Frage an die Christen," *ibid.,* pp. 604-15.

[2] Cf. T. Rendtorff and H. E. Todt, *Theologie der Revolution* (Frank-
furt/Main, 1968).

[3] Bibliographical references in *Dialogue between Christians and Marxists (Study Encounter,* Vol. IV, No. 1, 1968) (Geneva, World Council
of Churches).

[4] M. Machovec, *Marxismus und dialektische Theologie* (Zurich, 1965).

[5] J. Moltmann, *Theologie der Hoffnung* (Munich, ⁶1966).

[6] W. D. Marsch, *Hoffen worauf?* (Hamburg, 1963); G. Sauter,
Zukunft und Verheissung (Zurich, 1965), pp. 277-361; cf. the articles
by J. B. Metz, J. Moltmann, W. Pannenberg and P. Tillich in *Ernst
Bloch zu ehren* (Frankfurt/Main, 1965).

Motives for the Emergence of This Problem in Marxism

Is it correct to see Marxist thought as a special form of the question about the future? Certainly not if we are thinking only of traditional Marxism as established in an ideology of the power of the State. Marxists who are spokesmen of an intellectual opposition or agents of revolutionary movements behave differently: they do not have to commit themselves or justify things as they are, but can be flexible and appeal to novelty. Moreover, in many communist States disillusionment has crept in about social reality: the future that men were hoping for moves further away and becomes increasingly less palpable. During revolution, dream and reality were still one and remained interdependent. Once revolution was succeeded by the period of humdrum life, the dream fled before reality instead of penetrating it more deeply. In order to break out of torpor and resignation, the value for reality of the dream of a better life was rediscovered. Films like Purisa Djordjevic's *A Serbian Dream* or the works of Sergei Eisenstein are the aesthetic anticipation of the awakening of a new mentality. The Utopian mentality arouses hope that takes up the cause of human dignity against oppression by a world that is guided purely by external expediency. For a long time Marxists were regarded merely as advocates and agents of social and economic necessities. Today they are becoming more and more the exponents of a demand for the freedom that not only opposes every form of exploitation, but, with equal vehemence, rejects the tyranny of anonymous processes in a technically administered world. This makes Marxist views attractive even within the large Western industrial countries.

Misleading Presuppositions in the Dialogue

Changes in Marxism, and theological self-analysis, contradict the assertion that Marxism and Christianity from now on must rigidly face each other like two irreconcilable rival Churches. Two reasons are adduced, rather, for coexistence and cooperation—one religious and sociological, the other statistical. We are reminded first of all that the prophets of the Old Testament, like Jesus, upheld the cause of outcasts and the oppressed. It is argued from this that the biblical denunciations of the rich, the powerful and the Godless, are symptoms of social revolution. In addition, the history of the Christian sects that tried to fulfill the divine commandments radically, manifests kinship between the urgent Christian expectancy of the end of the world and the desire to change the world. The second occasion for rapprochement lies in foreseeable dangers in the political world. These compel all perceptive people to lay aside differences of opinion and cooperate in the humane formation of the future. Christians and communists are the two large groups in the world who promise to answer man's question about the meaning of life and of history. For this reason they are especially called upon to cooperate. These two reasons may well stimulate dialogue between them; they cannot be arguments against dialogue. Historical summaries, especially when designed to evoke admissions of guilt, run astray in protestations and wishful thinking, which obscure the material that could be brought into a dialogue. Forced interpretations of sayings of the prophets and of the message of Jesus likewise hold as little promise of expert agreement as does a perversion of theology into the sociology of religion.

Prospects for the Dialogue

The sense of solidarity and the need for communication may form the basis of dialogue, but cannot themselves become the content of a discussion that hopes to turn into dialogue—that is, to agreement in a truth that is sought in common. If each partner remains firmly tied to his own inherited outlook and system of convictions, all that is possible is the setting aside of historically generated differences in favor of new practical tasks, or at least the deferment of theoretical clarification. Then the binding force of what is common cannot any longer be expounded by argument, but must coincide with the affirmation of actual agreement. This gives rise to a crippling monotony which is nonetheless able to create reflexes focused upon slogans. The word "dialogue" possesses a curious magic that is escaped only in the direction of new obligatory freedoms. Freedom is the thing we must speak of here, because agreement is not possible on the basis of insights that are open to every intelligent and reasonable man. We are concerned, rather, with convictions that require personal assent and that are the fruit of an intellectual and in-controvertible decision.[7] The truth that is sought in such a di-alogue—intent upon reaching a binding conviction—is, as it were, a pole in whose field of force people are drawn together, although they have not set out from a common point. It might be obected that this is a flight into the future, in the hope of finding there what the present and the past deny. This objection falls away only when the heritage of divisive convictions is no longer felt as mere prejudice, but as something containing material for the future, that would be withheld by any fixation at a previous state of the discussion. In this the theologian will have to speak of the future of God—if possible, not with brash confessional bluntness but so that the reality of this future becomes plain, within the question that is freely being discussed. Dialogue is not a sermon. It occurs where the preacher is denied an audience, but where there is a readiness, an interior necessity, to listen to one another. This seems to be one of the signs of our times.

Changes in the Image of Atheism

In this context we cannot ignore the problem of atheism. Essential parts of Marxism emerged out of the 19th-century attack upon religion. Because of this ancestry it is attributed to atheism, and thus it has understood itself, for it represented a total view of the world from which God was excluded to make room for man. In so doing it does not mean to deny the existence of God theoretically and in general. What it denies is that God is the transcendent cause of the world: the creation and providence of God, which restricts the creative activity of man by connect-ing all far-reaching planning to primeval conditions. Again, it

[7] D. Dubarle, "Dialogue and the Philosophy of Dialogue," in *Convergence* 1 (1968).

denies that God is the transcendent motivator of all morality: God as the guarantor of a moral order of the universe, who prevents the erection of new values and who allows the future to be predetermined by the values of previous history. This suggests that we must see the characteristic platform of atheism as the protest against the future as the future of God. Before we discuss this any further, we must take note of the reappraisal of atheism by some Protestant theologians.

This assessment is connected with a return to the examination of Hegel's philosophy, seen as the *mediation* between theology and philosophy, between theism and atheism. Feuerbach had already explained that Protestant theologians would have "to become Hegelians, *de jure,* in order to be able to combat atheism".[8] Hegel's philosophy, however, is not regarded as a genuine reconciliation between non-Christians and Christians, but merely as the expression of a non-explicated co-existence, of a unity of faith and unbelief.[9] There arises, therefore—and this is repeated today—a sense of community, based upon the experience of the absence of God in our world (the "death of God"), and which supposes that the presence of God was directly available to the experience of former ages. The common consciousness of the times then demands a common language and denies theology the right to have a language and mode of thought of its own. In the process, language sinks to the level of information. Proof of the existence of God is now sought only in the assumption of a utopian conceptual system, which man is able to realize, thus gaining a share in the becoming of God in the world.[10]

Absolute Future

The possibilities of historical becoming are, however, also the point of attack of modern Marxist criticism of religion. As formerly, so today it rejects the Christian faith, insofar as it pre-

[8] L. Feuerbach, "Vorläufige Thesen zur Reform der Philosophie," in
[9] L. Feuerbach, "Grundsätze der Philosophie der Zukunft," *ibid.,* p. 176.
Kleine Schriften (Frankfurt/Main, 1966), p. 139.
[10] J. Moltmann, *op. cit.,* pp. 150-55.

vents man from attaining a mature awareness of himself, thus putting a barrier in the way of progress. Denial of God is made in the interests of foreseeable further development of man in an unforeseeable period of advancing time full of historical possibilities. Future thus means *futurum,* the dimension in which man is able to transcend himself, and to discover his own true form. The Christian, however, understands the future chiefly as the *adventus*, "an act of God that comes to meet him and calls him".[11] Future is not, therefore, the far-off present, but erupts into the present. "It must be the absolute fullness of reality as the causal vehicle of the dynamic of the future." [12] Precisely thus is God the "absolute future" that can never be exactly coincident with the advance of history. But the fact that God "implies a presence, a reality, whereas we only experience a postulate",[13] evokes contradiction from the Marxists.

The formula "absolute future" is the common denominator in the discussion. Although it seems to be a mere abstraction, for theologians it rests upon the biblically evidenced experience of God—of God who is neither the power of ancestry, nor the confirmation of the present, but the God of promise and of hope, because he leads men further on through time. God contradicts history that is self-contained and conceived as the continuation of a holy past (Is. 43, 18-19). God is the God who is coming (Ex. 3, 14). The Marxist understands the future as unlimited being. "Transcendence is the experience through which man attains the awareness of himself as God in becoming." [14] Here God is conceived as the definition of infinite man; he is drawn into the *futurum* of history; he becomes the embodiment of becoming. *Futurum* and *adventus* merge indistinguishably into one another.

[11] R. Garaudy, "De l'Anathème au Dialogue," in *Der Dialog* (Hamburg, 1966), p. 87.

[12] K. Rahner, "Marxistische Utopie und christliche Zukunft des Menschen," *ibid.,* p. 15.

[13] R. Garaudy, *op. cit.,* p. 89.

[14] R. Garaudy, "Christentum und Marxismus—heute," in *Gespräche der Paulus-Gesellschaft* (Vienna, 1966), p. 86.

Changing the World

Marxists, like Christians, do not allow the question about the future to slip out of the present, but draw it deeper into the present. This practical attitude to the present has been traditionally described in Marxist language as "changing the world". It is important for us to observe how this concept itself has changed. Pre-Marxist revolutionary tradition applied the concept to the destruction of the present order with the object of erecting a new order. For Marx, following Hegel, "changing the world" meant translating a philosophy of the absolute man, who fully comprehends the nature of the universe, into a political reality. Today Marxism has to yield to a concept of science which does not allow the unalterable reflection of data in perception, but which takes account of the reciprocal interaction of subject and object. It works with schemes, the validity of which is not established *a priori,* but has to be verified in application; it works with hypotheses and with models. Changing the world can be accomplished only within this framework and by these methods. This excludes all rigid socio-economic theory, especially if it affirms its political realization and regards the technical revolution as a mere by-product, having no reaction upon ideology. The concept, which the slogan "changing the world" must grow into under the influence of the principles of modern scientific theory, opens up fresh possibilities of an understanding between Marxists and Christians, in respect of empirical study. For, in guiding its schemes, this requires a picture of its objectives if it is to enjoy future development; in addition, the ideas linked with these objectives are never morally neutral, and hence involve the acceptance of some particular view of the nature of man. The problem of prognosis is no longer a special case, but the fundamental problem of knowledge, which cannot be solved without man's free answer.

The Merit of Marxism

In contrast to every other social doctrine, Marxism has a

start in the search for what is human in reality. Its theory takes account of contradictions in reality, expounds them and sharpens them by formalizing them. In this way it stands in contrast to organic, as to mechanistic, functionalism, both of which have molded the character of Western society and science. Organic functionalism can be traced back to classical mythology, occurs in the notion of universal harmony, and has been revived by Romanticism. It takes the view that man and the world, man and society, cooperate in an ordered interplay, that their actions interweave organically and balance out, in the long run. The mechanistic functionalism of the natural and historical sciences sees reality as a regulated sequence of events, which can be deduced in terms of cause and effect. All contradictions can be explained and hence set aside by attributing to them a dependence within the totality of this context. In both cases, what does not fit is integrated as unrest into the clockwork of life. By contrast, modern Marxism, in spite of its closeness to both of these viewpoints, regards itself as the advocate of all that must be maintained and worked out as contradiction in order to make possible something new. It remains true to what is dissonant, truculent and uneven, in order to preserve and develop this area as the sphere of what is characteristically human.

As a freedom movement this type of Marxism is in many ways akin to the origins of Christianity, which intellectually rejected the classical cosmos. Today Marxists are at pains to obtain a more precise observation of human behavior, in order to recognize the presuppositions and limits of human freedom. No picture of reality is possible without this knowledge. At this point dialogue begins to be sought with the Christian Churches, with their centuries-old experience of the assessment and the guidance of men. Marxists and Christians share a common inquiry into deep anthropological problems.

The Problem of Totality

The Christian picture of man is determined by knowledge about the beginning and end not only of human life, but of history. The finitude of created things is not a peripheral concern of human life, but is evident all the time. It is characteristic of the Christian faith that it tries to understand every individual in relation to the totality of a time that has a specific beginning and end. Beginning and end do not, however, mean simply temporal start and finish, but express a totality that goes beyond this experience: the totality of the revelation of God. Human experience cannot—to say the least—outstrip this revelation; possibly it cannot even get as far. This is what the term "absolute future" conveys. The absolute future is not detached from this present life, but erupts into this life, urging on this life's experience. As the history of the Church testifies, this experience encounters things unforeseen and unplanned. Openness to such unexpected experiences will provide a decisive contribution to the discussion about the future.

In the dialogue between Christians and Marxists, the concept of "absolute future" stands for the totality that is presupposed in every momentary experience. The problem of the revolutionary change of reality challenges the minds of Marxists in respect to a totality of history, an ultimate state of society. This state is not supposed to end history, but allows unreserved establishment within history. To achieve this condition, the totality of all possible experience must be anticipated. Only then can reality be so planned into the dimension of the future as to result in a development toward this totality. This relationship between totality, possible experience and already completed experience determines practical, world-changing action. It determines to what extent something that has already been achieved is acceptable or not. Interest in this relationship is—it would seem—the chief motive for the readiness of Marxists to enter into conversation with Christian theologians.

Donal Flanagan/*Maynooth, Ireland*

Eschatology and
the Assumption

"Wherefore, having directed humble and repeated prayers to God, and having invoked the light of the Spirit of truth, to the glory of almighty God, who has bestowed his special bounty on the Virgin Mary, for the honor of his Son, the immortal king of ages and victor over sin and death, for the greater glory of his august mother, and for the joy and exultation of the whole Church, by the authority of our Lord Jesus Christ, of the blessed apostles Peter and Paul, and by our own, we proclaim, declare and define it to be a dogma revealed by God that the immaculate mother of God, Mary ever Virgin, when the course of her earthly life was finished, was taken up body and soul into the glory of heaven." [1]

It is now possible to see the definition of Mary's assumption to glory as an end and a beginning. The dogmatic definition of what was conceived as Mary's final privilege marked, in fact, the effective end of a period of theological concentration on Mary in isolation.

There was a certain separation of the assumption, itself an eschatological affirmation, from the general treatment of eschatology. A more serious divorce, however, was at the basis of this failure to integrate the assumption into general eschatology—the theological isolation of Mary and the Church. This

[1] *Acta Apostolicae Sedis* (AAS) 42 (1950), 770.

has endured for a long time and is only now being slowly and painfully overcome.

The year of the assumption definition, 1950, has greater claim to be considered a turning point in the modern theology of Mary than 1958, the year of Pope Pius XII's death. It marks the real term of the Marian movement—in large measure an assumptionist movement at the popular level—of the 19th and early 20th centuries. With the definition the way was opened for a theology of Mary which could see itself radically as a doctrine on the Church.

The assumptionist movement of the 19th and early 20th centuries, out of which the definition came, and whose slow, steady advance may be followed in the stream of petitions directed to the Holy See from the accession of Pius IX, showed little or no sense of awareness of the Mary-Church analogy and the ecclesial significance of the truth of the assumption. In fact the whole process in which the doctrine came to be defined is marked by a concentration on the assumption as a Marian privilege and by an apparent unawareness of the ecclesial dimension of the doctrine. The dogmatic definition itself shows these same characteristics. This definition was nonetheless the decisive step back to an ecclesially oriented Mariology.

The section of the Apostolic Constitution *Munificentissimus Deus* which immediately precedes the solemn definition deals with the opportuneness of defining the assumption. It mentions several reasons favoring definition but does not specifically point to the theological relationship of Mary and the Church. It expresses, it is true, the hope "that faith in the bodily assumption of Mary into heaven may make our faith in our own resurrection both stronger and more active",[2] but it does not appear to advert to the exemplar character of the assumption itself for the individual or for the community of salvation. This reflects the narrow line of Marian thinking within which the definition came to be made.

[2] *Ibid.*

Many Catholics and many Protestants at the time of the definition had no clear grasp of the ecclesial meaning of the assumption. On the Protestant side, extremist reaction saw in the definition one more step in the Romish process of deifying the Virgin,
while more sober critics tended to emphasize the lack of scriptural foundation for the truth. It seems to have been accepted
that the assumption was an isolated *Marian* truth, not at the most
basic level a truth about the salvation of men. Catholics also at
this time were seeing the assumption in a very narrow framework. The mainly moralistic grounds for opportuneness which
the pope advances certainly give no indication that he saw the
definition as ushering in a new era in Mariology in which concentration would change from Mary as individual to Mary as
principal member of the Church.

The definition nonetheless gave Marian studies an objectively
ecclesial orientation. The suddenness and force with which the
theme Mary and the Church made its appearance—rather its
reappearance—in theological writing after 1950 is indeed rather
extraordinary.

Situating the Definition: 1950-1958

The assumption definition represents the end of a process
within the Church, a process in which a certain insight about the
Blessed Virgin Mary gradually emerged with full clarity as believed by the Church to be a revealed truth. The definition stated
the fact of the assumption. It did not at all go on to analyze its
theological implications in the fields of ecclesiology, anthropology and eschatology. This process got properly under way only
after the definition. In this writing the assumption was portrayed
not as an isolated Marian truth but as a truth which had a very
definite relevance for general soteriology. It was a truth which
said something concrete about Christian salvation, and about its
realization in man and in the Church.

There is a considerable distance from *Munificentissimus Deus*
to *Lumen Gentium,* chapters 7 and 8. This is immediately obvi-

ous if one compares the encyclical with, for example, n. 68 of *Lumen Gentium*. Both the shortcomings and possibilities of *Munificentissimus Deus* appear when it is read in the light of chapters 7 and 8. It is possible to see in the difference between these two documents the progress that theological understanding of the assumption has made between the definition and the present.

Analysis of the Definition

The definition speaks in terms of Mary's body and soul: "We proclaim and define it to be a dogma revealed by God that the immaculate mother of God, Mary ever Virgin, when the course of her earthly life was finished, was taken up" [3] *body and soul* to heavenly glory.

It is often assumed that these words, in denying an intermediate state for Mary's body, affirm this state for all other men. This thought must be examined.

When we attend to the defining words themselves, we find that what happens to other human beings on death is not under consideration. These words of the definition concentrate themselves on the final lot of Mary. They offer us no direct comment on others. It is, therefore, unwarranted to presume that in settling the question of Mary's final state the Church has said the last word about the present state of all other men. Whatever the believing Church may have held on this point at the time of the assumption definition in 1950, the definition was not focused directly on this problem.

There is the further consideration that it was open to the framers of the definition formula to have qualified the assumption as an unique privilege given to Mary alone. They did not do this. One can reasonably give a certain significance to the absence from the defining formula of any assertion that the assumption is a unique privilege. This absence becomes, it might be suggested, more significant still when we compare the definition

[3] *Ibid.*

formula of the assumption with the words used by Pius IX in defining the immaculate conception. In the case of the latter truth, the pope qualified it with the words: *"singulari omnipotentis Dei gratia et privilegio."* [4] He seems clearly to have wanted to underline the unicity of the privilege. A comparison of the text of the bull *Sollicitudo omnium ecclesiarum* of Alexander VII (Dec. 8, 1661) [5] with *Ineffabilis Deus* (Dec. 8, 1854) [6] shows a change of emphasis and the replacement of the word *specialis* by *singularis*. Neither of these terms, however, occurs in *Munificentissimus Deus.*

The defining formula in not alluding to Mary's assumption as a unique privilege, as something proper to Mary alone, may have been influenced by the fact there is mention in Scripture—and as a consequence in patristic and medieval writers—of final destinies analogous to that of Mary. The Christian faithful were familiar with the story of Elias and also that of Henoch. They were also aware of the mysterious allusion in the Synoptics to the saints who rose and showed themselves in the holy city at the time of Christ's death.

There is, finally, a most interesting echo of the assumption definition in n. 48 of *Lumen Gentium,* in the chapter which deals with the eschatological nature of Christian life. Our death is described as *"expleto unico terrestris vitae nostrae cursu".* These words recall consciously or unconsciously the precise phrase which was chosen in the encyclical on the assumption to avoid going into the problematic of Mary's death—*expleto terrestris vitae cursu.* [7] Can we see here perhaps an invitation to try working out the meaning of general eschatology from the concrete defined truth of the assumption?

At any rate it is clear that neither the definition of the assumption nor the Christian tradition (using the word in its broadest

[4] H. Denzinger-A. Schönmetzer, *Enchiridion Symbolorum* 32 (Freiburg i. Br., 1963), 2803.
[5] *Op. cit.,* 2015.
[6] *Op. cit.,* 2803.
[7] *Op. cit.,* 3903.

sense) is exclusivist in attitude. Neither can be said to rule out a final state of glory for some men other than Mary now.

Assumption of Mary and Present Final Lot of Man

It can be argued, then, that the assumption definition does not deny the possibility that other Christians than Mary exist already in a final state of glory similar to hers. Can we go a step further and argue that not merely does the assumption definition not deny this possibility but that it positively suggests its fulfillment? Is it reasonable to see the defined truth of Mary's assumption as a basis from which one can argue to a similar present condition for other Christians who have entered into glory?

Mary is not redeemed in isolation but is the first of that great communion of saints within which salvation is given. This great mystery of communion is realized already on earth and comes to its final perfection in the world to come in the heavenly Church. The entire heavenly Church can be seen as the type of the earthly Church. The Church of glory, the heavenly Jerusalem, is joined to the earthly pilgrim Church and is its model. There is one great communion of life, and the community in glory presents to the members of that same community still in the pilgrim state the ideal of final achievement toward which the pilgrims strive.

The Blessed Virgin assumed to glory is traditionally pictured at the head of a great procession of martyrs, confessors and virgins, at the head of the great host of the saved. Thus we see in Mary, assumed body and soul to heavenly glory, the precise state toward which the pilgrim Church is moving. Mary portrays the end-state and is therefore the ideal or model of the earthly Church. In Mary, the perfect member of the heavenly Church, the final state of the earthly Church has already begun. As n. 68 of *Lumen Gentium* states: "The mother of Jesus, in the glory which she possesses body and soul in heaven, is the image and beginning of the Church as it is to be perfected in the world to come."

Mary is already in that state of perfection toward which the pilgrim Church aims. To call her "type" or "figure" of the Church underlines that she enjoys this state of perfection, precisely as the model of the Church which is being formed, the earthly Church. As the heavenly model of redemption, she contrasts strikingly with the struggling Church of earth. Yet, precisely because she is its God-given model, she appears as promise or certain hope to the pilgrim People of God who make up this Church of earth.

The "figure" or "type" belongs in the actual final state of redemption; its correlative the pilgrim Church belongs in that of redemption in process, in this world. It seems better, then, not to employ the terms "figure" or "type" to describe Mary's relation to the heavenly Church—this, basically, because it tends to obscure the difference of condition of the earthly Church and the heavenly Church. It is plain that Mary cannot be the model for both in exactly the same way. If Mary is the type of the pilgrim Church, it is precisely because it is on pilgrimage and she enjoys the fulfillment. But the heavenly Church is not on pilgrimage and already enjoys the fulfillment. To say that Mary is its "type" or "figure"—i.e., insofar as she is in possession of the fulfillment—might appear to suggest that the heavenly Church somehow does not enjoy the fulfillment—which is substantially false. Thus the use of "type" or "figure" of the relation of Mary to the heavenly Church appears somewhat out of context. It is perhaps desirable, then, to confine this expression "type" or "figure" to expressing the relationship of Mary to the pilgrim Church and to seek for some other term to express the different relationship Mary has to the heavenly Church.

We should therefore view Mary and the heavenly Church as one. We should see Mary in and with the heavenly Church as the model, type and figure of the pilgrim Church. For the Church of glory is not complete without Mary, and in her it finds its most perfect expression or summary. In its totality the heavenly Church is the type of the pilgrim Church. It, the "cloud of witnesses" placed before us, is preeminently the bride, the New Jerusalem.

Mary and the Church of Glory

The expression "type" or "figure", while stressing a future identity or assimilation of the earthly Church and Mary, underlines at the same time their present disparateness of situation. There is a sharp and basic difference of condition between the model Mary and the earthly Church. Mary is in glory; the Church, a pilgrim, is "away from the Lord" (2 Cor. 5, 6). We find, nonetheless, in many of those who down the centuries have contributed to our present theological understanding of the theme Mary-Church, emphasis on the identity of Mary and the Church. This is perhaps most strikingly seen in the medieval tendency to interchange Marial and ecclesial titles.

Among common titles is "spouse", originally an ecclesial title in Scripture but gradually adopted as a title for Mary in a certain tradition of medieval writing, notably in the 12th century in the West. This term is interesting, first, because its adoption as a Marian title indicates a certain sense of an identity felt to exist between Mary and the Church. The use of this term, indeed the whole system of transference, indicates a developed grasp of the oneness of Mary and the Church.

This sense of the oneness of Mary and the Church is underlined in the same 12th century in the emergent Marial exegesis of the Canticle of Canticles. The "triple exegesis" was clearly the work of scholars to whom it came quite naturally to understand, read and see Mary and the Church portrayed under one and the same biblical figure. Further, it is clear from their attempts to integrate the Marial exegesis with the previously accepted ecclesial, individual exegesis that it was not intended to displace this exegesis. The Marial exegesis was to be fitted into the pattern of the ecclesial exegesis. Because of the similar basic direction of the two, this was possible. Mary was the special case within the general ecclesial sense. She did not deny the ecclesial meaning but affirmed it when her special relation to the Church was properly understood. This Marial-ecclesial exegesis of the Canticle thus brings out that in 12th-century writers there existed a certain highly developed sense of the unity of Mary and the Church which found particular expression in the symbol of the bride.

Parallel to the Marial exegesis of the Canticle we find in the same 12th century in liturgical texts and homilies a wealth of bridal imagery connected with the feast of the assumption. This is not really surprising in view of the fact that very often in the Christian tradition bridal imagery has an eschatological reference. It is, however, interesting to find the identification of Mary and the Church being propounded with such emphasis in this century under a symbol whose basic reference is eschatological. It appears that these writers saw Mary and the heavenly Church in very close relationship. The symbol "bride" which underlines identity belongs preeminently in the eschatological perspective. The Church as bride is before all the heavenly Church.

Apocalypse 12

A most interesting Scripture text often employed by Marian writers dealing with the assumption is from Apocalypse 12: "A great sign appeared in heaven, a woman clothed with the sun." This text in many of its interpretations in the Marian tradition seems to point in the same general direction of the identification of Mary and the Church in an eschatological perspective as did the 12th-century evidence just considered.

The woman "clothed with the sun" may be seen as describing under one symbol the heavenly Church and the Blessed Virgin Mary in this glorified Church. The woman "clothed with the sun" is definitely an ecclesial image and is certainly not the Blessed Virgin Mary in isolation. Yet the Marian traits discoverable in the passage lead authors to write that "the great sign is Mary as the Church" [8] and that "St. John under the figure of the woman in Apocalypse 12 portrays Mary as the Church".[9] It does not thus seem possible to say that the woman represents the Church, without reference to Mary.

[8] H. Müller, *Ecclesia—Maria* (Freiburg, ²1955), p. 228.
[9] B. J. Le Frois, *The Woman Clothed with the Sun,* (Rome, 1954), p. 262.

These indications lead us to suggest that if Mary in and with the Church of glory should be viewed as the type of the pilgrim Church, and if we are to see her relation to the Church of glory as somehow an identification, it must be an identification which yet allows her distinction from the Church of glory to appear.

Mary must always be viewed in a representative role. She is not a proxy; she, is, however, a personal representative of the community in which she is. This principle of representation familiarly applied in the Marian tradition to Mary's office at the incarnation and at the cross is verified most of all in the assumption. For in her assumption she *is* the Church in its final state and the type of the pilgrim Church.

The precise reason we can say that she *is* the Church is because of the nature of her representation. She is the typical member of the Church or the member who incorporates in her own person the whole of the Church. She is a personal paradigm of the final community of salvation. She is that community personalized or "impersonated" or made present in the one member who truly epitomizes it. Mary assumed incorporates in her own person the glorious Church, whose perfect and personal expression she is. In her this heavenly community is fully presented to us in its most perfect and most representative member. Mary then is not the "type" of the heavenly Church but its "impersonation" or its personal expression in her assumption. She expresses what this Church is, not what it will be.

Once we accept the point that Mary's relation to the Church of glory is that of a representative individual incorporating the collectivity in her person, it is plain that certain conclusions as to the present state of the Church of glory can follow. We may reasonably argue for a similarity of state in Mary and in the other members of the heavenly Church. If Mary is the personal model of the glorious Church, then ideally the one same state of the Church glorified will be verified in Mary and in the elect. Mary's assumption looked at in this way represents in a most clear fashion the actual state of the heavenly Church, whose "impersonation" she is. She is not the personification of a future state of this heavenly Church, but the personal expression of the present state of the collectivity, which is the heavenly Church. She is most closely identified with the saints in glory in one glorified community, yet she is differentiated from this community as its unique, complete, perfect, personal expression or "impersonation".

The eschatological perspective allows the greatest scope for an identification of Mary and the Church. Yet Mary appears quite clearly in this eschatological perspective as the *summa ecclesiae*. She and no one else incorporates personally the eschatological Church as redeemed and shows its actuality forth in her own person. She alone is the perfect "impersonation" of the community of salvation in its final form. Mary's uniqueness is not endangered by stressing her oneness with the Church of glory. Her special and unique relationship to the Church of glory as its "impersonation" obviates this.

Mary assumed is, therefore, with the Church of glory the model set before the pilgrim Church. She is the "impersonation" of the present state of the Church of glory. She expresses the future state of the pilgrim Church, the present state of the heavenly Church.

Mary is the "image and beginning of the Church as it is to be perfected in the world to come" (*Lumen Gentium,* n. 68). This need not be interpreted to mean that as yet this perfection is only given in Mary. Whether we see the Church of glory as already enjoying the final fulfillment in all its members or not, it remains true that Mary as the first and privileged member of this community may be designated not only as the image but as the beginning of the Church as it is to be perfected in the world to come. The privileged beginning of final glory we find in Mary in no way necessarily excludes the attainment of final glory by those others who belong to the heavenly Church even now.

Conclusion

As it is normally taken, Church teaching on the assumption seems to confirm the thesis of an intermediate state and to set the resurrection of the body at the last day. Man in glory before the last day emerges as separated soul while Mary appears as a fully redeemed human being.

The definition of November 1, 1950 concerns itself formally with the present state of the blessed Virgin Mary alone: it makes no explicit affirmations or denials about the present state of the rest of the human race.

The definition in its formal teaching in no way rules out the view that the rest of mankind enjoys even now the same final state of glory in the same way that the Blessed Virgin does. In fact, it might even be said to suggest positively that this is the case.

Mary glorified is traditionally seen in association with the communion of saints, as first of the redeemed, at the head of angels and saints; she is also traditionally seen as the type of the Church.

Mary's role of type of the Church is verified most aptly in relation to the earthly Church. It is better not to term her type of the heavenly Church because this seems to obscure the difference of condition between the pilgrim Church and the heavenly Church.

The heavenly Church as a whole, summed up in its most perfect member, Mary, is the prototype of the earthly Church. Mary, assumed, exemplifies the redeemed life as this is already enjoyed by the saints in glory even now. We who are "at home in the body" see the existence which is to be ours placed before us. This final state has been attained in Christ not only by Mary but by those who are with the Lord (cf. 2 Cor. 5, 6).

This understanding of the assumption underlines very sharply its eschatological significance and lets its definition appear as the means of a breakthrough to a new understanding of the relationship between "this side" and "the other side".

PART III
DOCUMENTATION
CONCILIUM

Office of the Executive Secretary
Nijmegen, Netherlands

Concilium General Secretariat/*Nijmegen, Netherlands*

Utopia

It seems a paradox that while many priests hesitate about speaking on eschatological topics, as has been pointed out in the Preface, the number of articles and books that deal with utopia as a phenomenon is constantly increasing.[1] This way of stating the position implies a certain affinity between eschatology and utopia. There is indeed a close link between the two, as the overall information contained in this article will show.

Therefore, here we need a brief historical orientation on this utopia; otherwise it might be understood as simply another word for unreality or a dream world, since such is the meaning the word has in current use. In the West, however, the word "utopia" has taken on a far more powerful meaning since Thomas More's *Utopia*[2] which appeared in 1516 in Louvain, and since

[1] An extensive bibliographical survey can be found in H. Süssmuth, *Studien zur Utopia des Thomas Morus* (Münster, 1967), pp. 169-86; O. Bucci, "Il secreto dell' Utopia," in *Renovatio* 3 (July-Sept., 1968), pp. 542-60; G. Picht, *Prognose, Utopie, Plannung* (Stuttgart, 1967); *Vom Sinn der Utopie* (Zürich, 1964); H. Schulte Herbrüggen, *Utopie und Anti-Utopie* (Bochum-Langendreer, 1960); P. R. Allen, "Utopia and European Humanism," in *Studies in the Renaissance* 10 (1963), pp. 91-107; S. Quinzio, "Utopia ed escatologia," in *Renovatio* 3 (July-Sept., 1968), pp. 441-51.

[2] E. Surtz and J. H. Hexter, *The Complete Works of St. Thomas More* 4 (New Haven and London, 1965), CLXXXIII (Editions of Utopia): *De optimo reipublicae statu deque nova insula Utopia libellus vere aur-*

then the concept has passed through a whole historical development.[3] After this first historical section (I), the next part of this article will show that in modern works about thematic theology, ethics and psychology, and particularly about sociology and politics or ideology, the authors constantly seek to link their thesis with the peculiar categories implied in the idea of utopia. We shall therefore try to indicate certain new categories which might be of use in our approach to the eschatological reality (II). But this demands that we eliminate certain phenomena which appear on the periphery of this idea of utopia (III). On the basis of a few socio-political studies we shall try to indicate certain utopian ideas that are present in any social structure and which are clearly visible in that unlimited belief in progress, probably of American origin (IV). In spite of these negative elements, utopia seems to play a positive part in the building up of society (V) and to be particularly significant in the Church's attempt to establish a presence in this world (VI).

I

HISTORICAL ORIENTATION

It is not mere accident that the appearance of Thomas More's book which introduced the concept of utopia into Western thought coincided with that reform movement [4] which, in the field of religion, is linked with Luther but which also pressed for new views in the political and social field. It was also the age

---

eus, nec minus salutaris quam festivus. (In this translation the more easily accessible *Everyman* edition has been used: Everyman's Library, n. 461).

[3] J. Servier, *Histoire de l'Utopie* (Paris, 1967); J. Lameere and others, *Les utopies à la renaissance* (Brussels, 1963); S. L. Thrupp (ed.), *Millennial Dreams in Action* (The Hague, 1962); H. Conrad-Martius, *Utopien der Menschenzüchtung* (Munich, 1955); G. Ritter, *Machtstaat und Utopie* (Munich, 1940).

[4] R. Padberg, "Der Sinn der Utopie des Thomas Morus. Fragen der politischen Verantwortung des Christen am Vorabend der Reformation," in *Theologie und Glaube* 57 (1967), pp. 28-47; E. W. Böckenförde, "Die Entstehung des Staates als Vorgang der Säkularisation," in *Säkularisation und Utopie* (Stuttgart, 1967), pp. 75-94.

when new political structures sprang up and a new understanding of freedom began to break through.[5] On the surface,
Thomas More's book seems to be only concerned with a renewal
of the social order and the political structures. With his gentle
humor he criticized the existing structures and society by depicting a kind of ideal state: Utopia. The fictitious discoverer of
Utopia, Raphael Hythlodaeus, relates his findings and concludes
at the end of the second book: "Now I have declared and described unto you as truly as I could the form and order of that
commonwealth, which verily in my judgment is not only the best,
but also that which alone of good right may claim and take upon
it the name of a commonwealth or public weal. For in other
places they speak still of the commonwealth, but every man
procureth his own private gain. Here, where nothing is private,
the common affairs be earnestly looked upon. And truly on both
parts they have good cause so to do as they do; for in other
countries who knoweth not that he shall starve for hunger, unless
he make some several provision for himself, though the commonwealth flourish never so much in riches? And therefore he is
compelled even of very necessity to have regard to himself rather
than to the people, that is to say, to others. Contrariwise, there
where all things be common to every man, it is not to be doubted
that any man shall lack any thing necessary for his private uses,
so that the common store, houses and barns, be sufficiently
stored. For there nothing is distributed after a niggish sort, neither is there any poor man or beggar; and though no man have
anything, yet every man is rich." [6]

After Hythlodaeus, More's *alter ego,* has finished, More pre-
tends with humorous subtlety that he does not agree with him
and says: "Thus when Raphael had made an end of his tale,
though many things came to my mind which in the manners and
laws of that people seemed to be instituted and founded of no
good reason, not only in the fashion of their chivalry and in their

[5] P. Ricoeur, "Approche philosophique du concept de liberté religieuse," in *L'Herméneutique de la liberté religieuse* (Paris, 1968), esp.
pp. 217 and 224.

[6] Everyman's ed., pp. 130-31; Yale ed., p. 236.

sacrifices and religions and in other of their laws, but also, yea, and chiefly, in that which is the principal foundation of all their ordinances, that is to say, in the community of their life and living without any occupying of money (by which thing only all nobility, magnificence, worship, honor, and majesty, the true ornaments and honors, as the common opinion is, of common-wealth, utterly be overthrown and destroyed) . . . I took him by the hand and led him in to supper, saying that we would choose another time to weigh and examine the same matters and to talk with him more at large therein." [6a] This whole argument too obviously suits modern ideologies not to be eagerly exploited by socialists or Marxists.[7]

More made up the name of this ideal state by joining the Greek negative *ou* (no, not) to the Greek noun *topos* (place), so that it means "nowhere". Does this mean that his ideal state is nothing but the uncommitted fantasy of a bookish humanist? In spite of the gentle humor, it reflects too well the acute criticism of an England which More tried to reform by his political in-volvement. The idea to write this *Utopia* probably came to him when in December 1515 he was sent by Henry VIII to Antwerp in order to negotiate a trade agreement with a delegation of Charles V. The first book of *Utopia* in particular sharply criti-cizes the social conditions of contemporary England. He was moved to write this book above all by the scandalous exploita-tion of those who were economically in a weak position. More was far more committed than his friend Erasmus to the correc-tion of social evils and the creation of a decent human existence for his depressed countrymen. The Dutch historian Huizinga was right when he said that More never meant to preach a kind of revolution that would lead to an earthly paradise. Nevertheless, More's *Utopia* comes closer to a practical program than either

[6a] Everyman's ed., p. 135; Yale ed., p. 244.

[7] Thus, e.g., K. Kautsky, *Thomas Morus und seine Utopia* (Stuttgart, 1887) and E. Bloch, *Freiheit und Ordnung. Abrisz der Soxial-Utopien* (N.Y., 1946), pp. 62-70; E. L. Surtz, *The Praise of Pleasure, Philosophy, Education and Communism in More's Utopia* (Cambridge, Mass., 1957); K. Mannheim, *Ideologie und Utopie* (Frankfurt am M., 1952).

Plato's *Republic* or St. Augustine's *City of God*. It owed its suc-
cess, however, less to its practical viability or its social and political program than to its urge to reform. To appreciate it only for
its literary qualities is not doing justice to the real value of this
work; it shows what man can do and expresses it in such a way
that even today those involved in the human sciences are fasci-
nated by it. G. K. Chesterton sensed this when he wrote that
More is of greater importance today than in his own time, "but it
is possible that after a century he will be considered the greatest
Englishman or at least the greatest historical character in English
history".

More's vision is characteristic of a specific kind of utopia.
Mesnard has described it [8] as a successful utopia to which the
West has remained faithful since the Renaissance in spite of all
religious, political and social changes. This utopia flows from a
kind of demand which is an integral and perhaps even an essential part of the human condition: the demand for more justice
and freedom, the basic principle of all reforms and all political
progress, an impelling influence the concrete positive aims of
which may be vague but which nevertheless inspires our judgment of the concrete situation by which we can express not what
is unreal, but rather what is more than real, what is better than
the present reality. Utopia, too, seems to be subject to historical
reality and yet it unleashes a force which moves irresistibly beyond the real, not toward the purely imaginary, but toward the
suprareal, to what lies beyond reality, beyond history and beyond our present experience of reality.[9]

One can trace this positive element in More's *Utopia* when
one compares it with other utopias. For he is neither the first nor
the only one to have attempted such an utopia. Since More
was a humanist, literary criticism has obviously referred to the
influence of Plato's dialogue about the State,[10] although Plato

[8] P. Mesnard, "L'Utopie de Robert Burton," in *Les Utopies à la Renaissance* (Brussels, 1963), pp. 75-88.
[9] R. Mucchielli, "L'Utopie de Thomas Morus," *ibid.*, p. 101.
[10] The study of More's sources is still far from complete. R. P. Adams,
in *The Philosophic Unity of More's Utopia*, says on p. 45: "Compre-

already saw influential utopians in Pythagoras and Hippodamos of Milete.[11] In fact, More himself quotes Plato, although more frequently in the first book which he wrote after he had rather hurriedly finished the second. And while there is a certain correspondence in details, the main ideas differ. When More planned the life of the community, he aimed at all mankind, while Plato only addresses himself to the upper classes. Plato reserves the benefits of this ideal state to a contemplative elite who are dispensed from all manual labor that remains the lot of the slaves. In Utopia practically all the members of the community have to work. In Plato harmony is ensured by subordinating everything to one idea. In Utopia there is genuine freedom, and harmony is the fruit of the moral effort of all. Plato does not seem to doubt that his ideal state can be put into practice without delay, while More knows that his plans cannot be realized at once but that his vision of Utopia will produce the corrective and stimulating force which is necessary.

More says explicitly that his *Utopia* is not the fruit of exaggerated mariners' tales but of human effort. When he wrote *Utopia*, literature was full of tales of mariners who on their voyages discovered all kinds of fancy islands. More lets his narrator take part in the voyages of Amerigo Vespucci,[12] but makes him then undertake a voyage of his own in the course of which he discovers the island of Utopia. Under this guise More then unfolds his own view of a state where everyone can be happy.

---

hensive treatment of the sources of Utopia is yet to be made." In his Introduction to the Yale edition (p. cliiif.), he lists the studies that have appeared so far, but concludes that L. Beger, "Thomas Morus und Plato. Ein Beitrag zur Geschichte des Humanismus," in *Zeitschr. für die gesamte Staatswissenschaft* 35 (1879), pp. 187-216, is still the best. The same holds for the influence of other classical authors such as Plutarch, Herodotus and Seneca. At most, one can see there the continuity of thought which More shaped in his work in an original and convincing way.

[11] E. L. Minar, *Early Pythagorean Politics in Practice and Theory* (Baltimore, 1942); Aristotle, *Politicon* II, 8.

[12] H. Süssmuth, *loc. cit.*, pp. 38f.; J. Grosset, "Two Notes on More's Utopia," in *Notes and Queries* (London, 1960), p. 366.

The Utopias before More may be described as "the conquest of the future, the subduing and exorcising of the future in order to force it to develop on the lines of a preconceived model",[13] or as the projection of an unlimited desire which does not ask for the real possibility but only for the ideal (K. Keréni). More's Utopia, however, must be described as a hope in man's capacities and in the possibility of an ethical renewal.[14] Before More most Utopias did not really aim at a renewal but reached back to an original situation, a piece of earthly paradise discovered somewhere on an island.[15] In fact, they look back and idealize the original state of man. This still holds partly for two well-known Utopias after More, that of Campanella[16] and that of Francis Bacon.[17] In the description of the "sun-state" (*citta del sole*) of the Dominican Tommaso Campanella (1568-1639), one is aware of a revolutionary undercurrent but ultimately his ideal state is the outcome of his idea of God and basically a preestablished reality which men must achieve preferably under the world dominion of the pope. The English thinker Francis Bacon founds the harmony of his ideal state, New Atlantis, first of all on the autonomy of the sciences. But for him, too, though inaugurating the period of enlightenment, this science is nothing but the recovery of the power man originally had over nature. Bacon, too, is convinced of man's ability to coordinate the sciences in such a way that he will recover the lost science of man's original state.

This idea of recovering or discovering paradise inspired even people like Columbus to set out on a search for a new world. When he went ashore in this new world, he was convinced that

[13] O. von Nell-Breuning, *Säkularisation und Utopie*, loc. cit., p. 239.

[14] J. Servier, *Histoire de l'Utopie* (Paris, 1967), p. 281.

[15] P. Secretan, "L'utopie comme symbole," in *Cahiers Intern. de symbolisme* 8 (1965), p. 52: "A utopia is a kind of synthesis of two disjointed universes: the violent and irrational universe of experience and the suprarational universe of sacred principles."

[16] A. Corsano, *Tomaso Campanella* (Bari, 1961); *Enciclopedia Cattolica* III, pp. 449-56.

[17] E. Gilson, *Les métamorphoses de la cité de Dieu* (Louvain-Paris, 1952); E. Cresson, *Francis Bacon* (Paris, 1956), p. 20; *The Works of Francis Bacon* III (Stuttgart, 1963), p. 40.

he had found the promised land of the Old Testament, not far from the original paradise. This conviction was so strong that he took a Jewish convert with him who knew Hebrew and Aramaic, Rodrigo de Jerez, because Columbus had not the slightest doubt that the inhabitants of his new world would speak this language.[18] More's Utopia, however, is plainly based on a view of the future and nowhere appeals to one or other original state of man. On the contrary, his ideal state is the result of human labor and ethical development. From this point of view his Utopia looks more like a secularization of the current view of heaven than a return to an earthly paradise; it is the conscious self-realization of an idealized but in no sense unattainable human community which has conquered the phase of individualism. And this Utopia marks a genuine step forward in man's self-realization, however many links there may be with Utopias that preceded or came after More's.

II

MODERN INTEREST IN MORE'S UTOPIA

Van Peursen has spoken about mythical truths that develop into ontological truths and then pass over into functional truths. Before him Comte had already held that man passed from a religious or theological phase into a philosophical phase, and from there into the scientific phase. All this presupposes that

[18] M. Eliade, "Paradis et Utopie," in *Eranos Jahrbuch 1963* (Zurich, 1964), p. 213; C. L. Sandford, *The Quest for Paradise* (Urbana, 1961), p. 40; G. H. Williams, *Wilderness and Paradise in Christian Thought* (New York, 1962): "God made me the proclaimer of the new heaven and the new earth mentioned in the Apocalypse of St. John after having been foretold through the mouth of Isaiah; he showed me the place where they could be found" (pp. 65f.). The evangelization of the United States also bore this eschatological mark. The Englishmen who evangelized the United States were convinced that God had held up the discovery of the new world until after Luther's Reformation so that it would only know the pure Gospel and not that Gospel which, according to them, was perverted into the message of the antichrist by Rome.

certain truths constantly acquire a new and different relevancy in history. It is possible that the aspect of truth, envisaged in More's Utopia, is becoming relevant again today as functional truth. One author has already referred to Harvey Cox's *Secular City* on these lines: Have we not here a truth which was formerly seen in mythical terms, reached the ontological phase with More's *Utopia* and now emerges again as a functional truth? [19] However this may be, the fact is that time and again More's Utopia recurs in modern studies. This happens for instance in psycho-analytical studies where Utopia is seen as the product of the power of man's limitless desire and the powerlessness of his creative strength.[20] It is pointed out at the same time that this utopia is one of the most powerful symbols through which man can express his faith in the future [21] so that man is as essentially *homo utopicus* (utopian man) as *homo faber* and *homo sapiens*. The assertion that there is no future for religion as confession but only as politics [22] seems to show a similar new appreciation of Utopia: what More saw as the ideal state modern man seems to accept as possible.[23] The socialist Kautsky sees in the Utopia the forerunner of the socialist state.[24] Oncken and Ritter [25] see in More a planner of genius and the prophet of the liberal politics of the future. Padberg [26] sees in Utopia the beginnings of a new awareness of Christian responsibility for the state and the first traces of the influence of public opinion in substituting the authority of freedom for that of power. From within this freedom the Christian is then able not merely to dabble in politics alongside of his Christian practice, but to fulfill his Christian mandate in his political

[19] P. J. Roscam Abbing, "Cox als theoloog," in *Wending* 23 (April, 1968), p. 131.

[20] J. Servier, *op. cit.*, p. 316.

[21] J. Arquer, "Kirche and der Leine der Revolution," in *Rheinischer Merkur* 39 (Sept. 27, 1968), p. 4.

[22] P. Antoine, "Démystifier la politique," in *Christus* 15 (Oct. 1968), p. 470.

[23] J. Servier, *op. cit.*, p. 201.

[24] H. Süssmuth, *op. cit.*, p. 2.

[25] *Ibid.*, p. 3; cf. n. 3.

[26] Cf. n. 4.

commitment (right, left or center) as the world in which he lives may demand.[27] The *eschata* (the ultimate realities) need then no longer be seen in terms of a temporal before and after (before and after my life, before and after the Church), but rather in categories of quality: can we not reduce the "endlessness" of our desire, provisionally expressed in utopias, to concrete proportions, and how far is this desire and consequently the Christian hope only the frustration of an originally creative power or a camouflaged substitute for the satisfaction of sexual and aggressive urges? As Ricoeur said, is it not possible to give a progressive interpretation of this desire, aiming at a concrete future reality, as well as a retrogressive one, back to paradise? Is Christianity a kind of dialectic between the progressive and the retrogressive interpretation?

In any case these observations should make the theologian circumspect when realities that used to be described with concepts such as heaven and hell are too easily reduced to mere psychological or social values and prevent him from being too profoundly impressed by the assertion that the desire of future happiness necessarily alienates man from himself. While heartened by the liberating accents of Cox's *Secular City,* we should nevertheless ask ourselves whether he does not diminish the meaning of those concepts too much. As one critic puts it: "On reading these pages it becomes only too clear that, in spite of the outspoken modern ideas, the so-called secular city is still a city closely linked by a kind of bastard relationship with some other cities which provided a model for More's *Utopia,* namely the cities of Plato and Augustine." [28] The danger is then not wholly imaginary that the Secular City will be used to provide the Americans with an untroubled conscience which allows them to do what they do *de facto:* to summon God to execute all well-meant projects concocted by man; to play up to the pride of technicians, managers, statesmen and those that are revolutionary-

[27] J. B. Metz, "Disputa sull'avvenire dell'uomo," in *Sapienza Ital.* 20 (1967), pp. 141-54.

[28] G. van der Flier, "De civitate domini Coxii," in *Wending* 23 (April 1968), p. 113.

minded, all of whom "do what they can" to solve the problems of society while taking great care to protect their self-interests and their "safety".[29] The real force of Utopia is precisely that it can never rest content with the status quo and provides the energy to go forward in spite of the tragedy of human reality. If history must become salvation history, this can never come about by following an imitative interpretation of already existing history but only by a Christian involvement in that history which must still be made.

III
FRINGE PHENOMENA OF UTOPIA

The advantage of a Utopia in the growing self-awareness of mankind lies in its evocative character and the stimulus with which it encourages man to work for the future. But this reveals at the same time its vulnerability. As soon as a Utopia is pinned down to specific sociological, philosophical and theological notions, it loses its stimulating influence and becomes desirable as an object. A Utopia is by nature vague and therefore constantly threatened by ideology.[30] By ideology we understand a partial truth which wants to pass for the whole truth. The strivings of Utopia then become identified with the content of Utopia. The proper nature of an ideology is that it is a conviction which is believed to be evoked by reality but is in fact kept alive by the desire to satisfy individual interests. Utopia can only function as a literary story; as soon as it is taken for the reality it becomes an ideology. In this sense Marx is reproached today for having twisted More's Utopia to his own ideology.[31] Ideology will always tend toward one-sidedness. This was clear in the process which prevailed in the Enlightenment: rationalization of the reality is necessary, but as soon as it was identified with progress it

[29] S. S. Schwarzschild, "A Little Bit of Revolution?" in *The Secular City Debate* (New York, 1966), pp. 147-49.
[30] J. Hersch, *Die Ideologiën und die Wirklichkeit* (Munich, 1957).
[31] E. Topitsch, "Limites de la critique de l'idéologie," in *Rev. universitaire de science morale* (1966), p. 58.

began to show the one-dimensional character of an ideology. In this sense the God-is-dead theology also begins to show the character of an ideology.[32]

The notion of ideology always has the connotation of an impossible ideal. When ideology penetrates into Utopia, the Utopian becomes something of a fanatic because he will pursue this impossible ideal with every possible means. And so an ideology becomes a dogmatic whole which knows of only one ethic, one system of politics, one religious ideal. This jeopardizes an essential part of More's Utopia, namely, its tolerance (and also what has been called the logic of humor). The Utopian then begins to use the word "radical" which excludes doubt. This combination of Utopia and ideology occurs at every level of the human condition. It tends to sow the deadly germs of unreality in the living seed of Utopia.

Examples of such a contamination of Utopia by ideology can be found in both Christianity and Marxism. When, for instance, Marxism ridicules the Christian ideal of redemption by pointing to the necessary productivity of man in service of a state of salvation, one idealized Utopia (to be purely spiritual) is attacked with another (to be purely productive). González-Ruiz has developed this in an article in this volume of *Concilium*. When it is said that myths are not the truth but a summons to thought, the same must be said of utopias: they are never the truth of the future (as if the future will necessarily be as the utopias insinuate) but they are a constant urge to be involved in ethics and politics. Such realities as paradise, heaven, People of

[32] H. Cox, "Beyond Bonhoeffer? The Future of Religionless Christianity," in *The Secular City Debate* (New York, 1966), p. 209; E. Bloch, *Das Prinzip Hoffnung* (Frankfurt a. M., 1967), p. 67. All fatalism is alien to Christianity. Just as it could not rest content with the general conviction that God was alive, so it cannot rest satisfied with the fact that God "happens" to be dead and with accepting this fact fatalistically. In Bonhoeffer, hope was alive that the Christian faith would again have a formative influence on a world that had become mature if that faith was renewed through a reinterpretation of the Bible. This presupposes more than a mere statement or a mere interpretation. In the latter case the positive utopia would become "utopistic", lose its stimulating effect and kill the spirit.

God, and their opposites, desert, hell, pagans, always thrive on Utopias but become unreal when permeated by ideologies.

IV
SOCIAL AND POLITICAL ASPECTS OF UTOPIA

It is impossible to separate the social and political aspects contained in every Utopia, and very explicitly so in More's, from the other aspects, such as the cultural, literary or Judaeo-Christian ones. The social and political aspects of Utopia only come to the fore when the Utopia becomes really operative, as, for instance, in the Holy Roman Empire, the French Revolution (utopia of equality), Marxism (utopia of the classless society) or in Western society (utopia of the welfare state). It has been said that the origin of utopias is historically conditioned: historical evils always lead to utopias. This is partly true. But it is also true that the millennarianism which crops up regularly in Church history also produces utopias. Behind each utopia there always lies the urge toward renewal, regeneration and improvement to bring about the best possible world. Almost all the political systems that were inspired by a utopia started with a new calendar. The French Revolution, Fascism and Marxism begin with the year 1. The social and political aspect of a utopia is marked by a negative reaction to what went before. The Utopian will not adapt himself to the concrete elements of the society in which he lives; he wants to create a new order from which these elements are eliminated. Within Marxism some factors are systematically not mentioned, just as in Church history certain factors are hushed up, particularly in apologetic histories of the Church or of dogma. Instead of the existing society the Utopian wants to create an ideal society [33] where there is no room for evil and fear.

[33] On the flyleaf of Aldous Huxley's modern Utopia, *Brave New World*, there appears a quotation from Berdiaeff: "Utopias seem far more capable of realization than man thought in the past. Today we are faced with a far more worrying issue: How can we escape their

And so the ideal social and political man is presented as a limitless sublimation of humanity. Such a man is no longer opposed to human society in any sense because he identifies himself with that society; every difference and distinction is suppressed; he becomes purely social and his self-awareness totally conforms to that of the community so that there is no longer any room for a private life in any sector, religion included. In this sense the concept of the Church can also begin to function as a social-political utopia but is then exposed to the danger of every ideology, namely, to fall outside reality and to become an island. The most valid criticism of Marxism and ecclesiastical-ideological centralization is that which attacks this social and political aspect of political and religious ideology. In such a context science itself is subordinated to the utopia: one begins to plan a man who fits into this social and political utopia.[34] This encourages the utopian overestimation of science whereby a simplified concept of progress is given shape in the so-called welfare state.

V

THE POSITIVE FUNCTION OF UTOPIA

Accelerated after the 16th century, Utopia has penetrated into the whole of Western history. Is it a mere fringe phenomenon of

---

final realization? . . . Utopias can be achieved. Life is on its way towards utopias. Perhaps we are on the threshold of a new age in which the intellectuals and the educated classes will dream of means of avoiding these utopias and returning to a non-utopian age, less 'perfect' but with more freedom." Instead of humor our modern utopias are penetrated by a grim sarcasm, as e.g., in George Orwell's novel *1984*. Cf. the penetrating study by K. Spinner, "Utopische Romane aus England," in *Neue Züricher Zeitung* (March 10, 1963).

[34] H. J. Müller, "The Human Future," in J. Huxley, *The Humanist Frame* (London, 1962), p. 405. The biologists and geneticists themselves are not quite so optimistic about managing man himself; they do not yet see a superman but only some laborious variations on the theme of the old one. See W. Büchel, "Ist der Mensch konstruirbar?" in *Theologie und Philosophie* 43 (1968), p. 243.

this history or part of it? Is it only a literary phenomenon or is it part of Western man's language itself? [35] One cannot answer this question by simply pointing to a concrete result: the kind of little model state set up by the Jesuits at the conquest of Paraguay.[36] The scope of the influence of Utopia reaches far beyond the geographical boundaries of a specific territory. Nor will it do to point to the fact that modern sciences have been provided with a rough outline of the scope of their investigations in a pre-scientific stage (utopia is never a "logos").[37] The positive function of utopia should rather be sought in a qualitative change in the way man thinks about the future. Instead of an unconscious vague expectation there should appear a deliberate and conscious expectation of the future. This will influence thought, the collective image of the aim which mankind believes it is pursuing, and the decision-making of every day. In this way utopia exercises a positive influence on the building of the community. Neither economics, nor technology, nor science can ignore the factual functioning of utopias in our society.

This change in our attitude toward the future does not yet bridge the gap between utopia and practical reality.[38] The utopia of peace does not itself create the scientific apparatus and the ethic required to organize peace; the utopia of the one world does not abolish by itself the myth of sovereign nation-states or directly influence political decisions; the utopia of the equality of all men cannot by itself root out racial discrimination. If utopia is left to itself, it is difficult to prevent it from becoming a myth of the future where the irresponsible like to seek shelter. But it cannot be denied that this change in mentality has set things going in thought, in ethics and in sociology. Without the positive

[35] R. Schäfer, "Welchen Sinn hat es nach einem Wesen des Christentums zu suchen?" in *Zeitschr. f. Theol. u. Kirche* 65 (July 1968), p. 345.

[36] G. Furlong, *Misiones y sus Pueblos de Guaranies* (Buenos Aires, 1962); E. Cardozo, *Historiografía Paraguaya* I (Mexico, 1959).

[37] J. Servier, *L'Histoire de l'Utopie* (Paris, 1967), p. 367.

[38] C. F. von Weizsäcker, *Gedanken über unsere Zukunft* (Göttingen, 1966), p. 30.

influence of this utopia, scientific progress itself, even at its most rational and technical, would be impossible.

VI

THE SIGNIFICANCE OF UTOPIA FOR THEOLOGY

It has already been pointed out that psychologists of culture, such as Keréni, maintain that, from their specific angle, the expectations of the future as they appear in Judaism and Christianity are not religious utopias which can be reduced to psychologically assumed archetypes, as is the case with other utopias which find there their common root or matrix. This does not, however, make these utopias immune from the usual liability to fringe phenomena. That is why they must be constantly subjected to the criticism of theology and the practice of the faithful. Christian conviction, however, needs these utopias in order to change the face of the earth effectively, not by an outward projection of future expectations, but by building up an ethics which enables man to achieve the expectation of the future in his own person. Otherwise the expectation of the future becomes an exteriorized faith in progress and blind vitality. The more the qualities of utopia, renewal, regeneration, equality and hiddenness are projected outside the person, the more man will fall a prey to the very technical means he himself has produced and so land himself in an alienation which is far more fatal than that of religion.

Löwith [39] has shown that "promethean" man needs special and radical measures in order to escape destruction by the productive forces he himself has unleashed. With the help of this formless utopia, theological thought about the Christian expectation of the future will have to mold a form of hope which will appeal to contemporary man. How fruitful this work can be is shown in the work of Moltmann, who was inspired by the

[39] K. Löwith, "Verhängnis des Fortschritts," in *Die Idee des Fortschritts* (Munich, 1963), p. 36; cf. "Miszachten die Christen die Zukunft?" in *Herder Korrespondenz* 22 (July 1968), pp. 297-301.

utopian thought of Bloch.[40] The strength of Moltmann lies in that he shows how the "not yet" and the "still coming" of God's kingdom can provide a positive interpretation of what Bloch called "meta-religion" (like "meta-physics": what comes after religion: the communal commitment to that *humanum*, that truly human condition, which we have not yet discovered, and which functions as a utopian hypostatized ideal of the still un-known man). The question is then not whether Christianity *has* a future but whether it *makes* one and whether Christians can find a meaning for what they build up together with others, which is not a mere option. Christianity is not merely historical because it can relate its past but also because it knows something about its future and can express this intelligibly. History can no longer be identified with *Herkunftgeschichte,* a history of ori-gins.[41] The Christian cannot dispose of the future because this future is more than what he can make of it with other people. He experiences it always as something provisional,[42] but in his faith he knows that it will definitely come about through him who comes and who said of himself that he will make all things new.

[40] E. Bloch, *Das Prinzip Hoffnung* II (1959), pp. 1323, 1515 and 1521.
[41] J. B. Metz, "Der christliche Glaube und die Zukunft," in *Univer-sitas* (March 1968), p. 219.
[42] J. Thomas, "Pour des Utopies provisoires," in *Signes du Temps* 7-8 (1968), p. 25.

BIOGRAPHICAL NOTES

AUGUSTIN GEORGE, S.M.: Born in France in 1915, he was ordained in 1941. He studied at the Faculty of Theology in Lyon, France, at the Biblical Institute in Rome and at the Biblical College in Jerusalem. He gained his licentiate in biblical science and his doctorate in theology, and he is currently professor of the New Testament at the Faculty of Theology in Lyon. He collaborated on the *Jerusalem Bible,* and his publications include *L'Announce du Salut de Dieu! Evangile de Luc* (Paris, 1963).

PETER MÜLLER-GOLDKUHLE: Born in Germany in 1938, he was ordained in 1965. He studied in Germany at the universities of Bonn and Würzburg, and in Switzerland at the University of Fribourg, receiving his doctorate in theology in 1966. He is rector of St. Michael's in Oberhausen, Germany.

EDWARD SCHILLEBEECKX, O.P.: Born in Belgium in 1914, he was ordained in 1941. He studied at the Saulchoir and at the School of Higher Studies at the Sorbonne. He received his doctorate in theology, and is currently professor of dogmatic theology at the University of Nijmegen. His major publications in English translation include *Christ, the Sacrament of the Encounter with God, Mary, Mother of the Redemption, Marriage: Secular Reality and Saving Mystery, Vatican II: The Real Achievement,* and *The Eucharist.*

ENRICO CASTELLI GATTINARA DI ZUBIENA: Born in Italy in 1900, he is a Catholic. He studied at the University of Rome, receiving a doctorate in philosophy in 1924. He is professor of religious philosophy at the University of Rome, where he is also director of the Institute of Philosophic Studies. His important publications include *Existentialisme théologique* (Paris, 1966) and *Simboli e immagini. Studi di Filosofia dell'Arte sacra* (Rome, 1966).

ANTON GRABNER-HAIDER: Born in Austria in 1940, he was ordained in 1965. He studied theology at Graz, in Austria, and in Germany at the universities of Tübingen, Bonn and Münster. He received his doctorate in theology in 1965, and is currently professor of catechetics at the

Ecole Normale in Graz. His publications include *Paraklese und Eschatologie bei Paulus. Welt und Mensch in Anspruch der Zukunft Gottes* (Munster, 1968).

José-María González-Ruiz: Born in Seville in 1916, he was ordained in 1939. He studied in Rome at the Gregorian and the Biblical Institute. He received his licentiate in Sacred Scripture and his doctorate in theology, and was formerly New Testament professor at the major seminary of Malaga in Spain. He is the diocesan theologian in Malaga, and is also public relations officer for the diocese. His publications include *Marxismo y cristianismo frente al "hombre nuevo"* (Madrid, 1962) and *El Cristianismo no es un humanismo* (Barcelona, 1966).

Piet Schoonenberg, S.J.: Born in Amsterdam in 1911, he was ordained in 1939. He studied at the Faculty of Theology of Maestricht, Holland, and at the Biblical Institute in Rome. He received his doctorate in theology, and is professor of dogmatic theology at the University of Nijmegen. His publications in English translation include *Man and Sin* and *God's World in the Making*.

Samuel Rayan, S.J.: Born in India in 1920, he was ordained in 1955. He studied at the University College of Trivandrum in Kerala, India and at the Gregorian in Rome. He received his doctorate in theology in 1960, when he became bursar at Kerala University. He contributed "Dialoog met her Hindoelïsme" to *Missionaire wegen voor morgen* (Hilversum-Anvers, 1967).

Gerhard Sauter: Born in Germany in 1935, he is a member of the Evangelical Church, and was ordained a pastor in 1962. He studied in Germany at the Universities of Tübingen and Göttingen. He is a doctor of theology, and professor at the University of Mainz, Germany. His publications include *Zukunft und Verheissung. Das Problem der Zukunft in der gegenwärtigen theologischen und philosophischen Diskussion* (Zurich, 1965).

Donal Flanagan: Born in Dublin in 1929, he was ordained in 1955. He studied at the University Colleges of Dublin and Galway, at St. Patrick's College, Maynooth, and at the University of Tübingen. He received his doctorate in theology, and is professor of dogma and patrology at St. Patrick's College, Maynooth. He contributed an essay on "The Church and Our Lady" to *The Meaning of the Church* (Dublin, 1966), a book he edited and for which he wrote the Preface.

International Publishers of CONCILIUM

ENGLISH EDITION
Paulist Press
Glen Rock, N. J., U.S.A.
Burns & Oates Ltd.
25 Ashley Place
London, S.W.1
DUTCH EDITION
Uitgeverij Paul Brand, N. V.
Hilversum, Netherlands
FRENCH EDITION
Maison Mame
Tours/Paris, France
JAPANESE EDITION (PARTIAL)
Nansôsha
Tokyo, Japan

GERMAN EDITION
Verlagsanstalt Benziger & Co., A.G.
Einsiedeln, Switzerland
Matthias Grunewald-Verlag
Mainz, W. Germany
SPANISH EDITION
Ediciones Guadarrama
Madrid, Spain
PORTUGUESE EDITION
Livraria Morais Editora, Ltda.
Lisbon, Portugal
ITALIAN EDITION
Editrice Queriniana
Brescia, Italy